effective group discussion

John K. Brilhart
University of Omaha

WM. C. BROWN COMPANY PUBLISHERS
Dubuque, Iowa

Speech Series

Consulting Editor
Baxter M. Geeting
Sacramento State College

Copyright © 1967 by
Wm. C. Brown Company Publishers

Library of Congress Catalog Card Number: 67—21304

ISBN 0—697—04101—8

Sixth Printing, 1970

Printed in the United States of America

Dynamic developments of our time, particularly the communication explosion and new revelations concerning human behavior, demand fresh approaches to the teaching of speech. Modern life places an emphasis on speech as an *act of communication,* interdisciplinary in nature, capable of adding new dimensions to man's evolution and progress in all areas of life. The SPEECH COMMUNICATION SERIES, addressed to the introductory student, represents a significant attempt to provide new materials for today's teaching needs.

Basic to all titles in the series is the desire to present the material in the clearest and most lucid style for the purpose of making speech communication a useful, ethical and satisfying experience. While the individual titles are self-contained, collectively they provide the substance for a comprehensive study of those topics fundamental to a basic course in speech communication.

PREFACE

Effective Group Discussion was written for any person interested in becoming a better discussant and leader of small group discussions. Every attempt was made to keep it clear and meaningful to the beginning student rather than impressive to researchers or advanced students. While the book is expected to be used primarily for courses in fundamentals of speech and small group discussion, it should prove equally valuable to committee members and chairmen, businessmen and leaders of adult learning groups. This book may be combined with several others in the Brown Company series to provide a text for a basic speech course, to supplement a text in fundamentals of speech, or as the text for a first course in group discussion.

The chapter sequence follows closely the order in which the author usually introduces the various topics to a class in discussion. Some instructors may want to vary this order considerably. The chapters were written to permit such a rearrangement without any substantial loss in meaning.

This should be primarily a *practical* book, more a handbook than a work in theory. The exercises have all been used repeatedly in teaching discussion. All have proven useful, and have been so judged by students. Throughout the book the emphasis has been placed on techniques and approaches that have been useful and effective in the author's teaching of both college students and informal adult classes.

Although ideas have been drawn from a variety of sources, several innovations will be discovered. Extensive attention has been given to learning discussions, based on research not previously published. Special emphasis has been given to the techniques and values of feedback in interpersonal relations. Techniques for stimulating imagination and creativity, especially the Creative Problem-Solving Sequence, are developed in detail.

Writing this book brought to mind the debt I owe to many great teachers who interested me in discussion, social psychology and creative thinking, especially J. Donald Phillips, Elton S. Carter and Sidney J. Parnes. Many college students, participants in adult study-discussion groups and discussion leaders from businesses and unions made indirect contributions. Most of all, I am indebted to my wife, Dr. Barbara L. Brilhart, for her helpful criticisms and suggestions.

J. K. B.

CONTENTS

Contents

*effective
group
discussion*

Chapter 1

DISCUSSION IN OUR WORLD

The local chapter of the American Association of University Professors had met to listen to a panel discussion. Six members of the Student Council were helping the faculty understand the need for more student-faculty interaction outside of the classroom:

> Well, I wish I could get to know some of my profs as people, not just as teachers and experts.

> Yes. I mean, what is a prof's home like? How does he think and live as a person? Could I learn from or be guided by him?

> Last year we had a series of meetings with faculty members in their offices, but only a few students showed up. Do we really mean what we've been saying about wanting more informal contact with the faculty?

After finishing dessert, the family was talking around the table about a complaint Betty had lodged against her junior high school history teacher:

> Betty, how did your history class go today?

> Oh heck, Mom. Mr. Stonehenge said he didn't care what the Supreme Court had said, he felt we all ought to be reading our Bibles and going to church every Sunday.

> He did? Wait a minute. Just exactly what did he say?

> Well, Dad, as best I can recall it . . . .

The scene was the office of the vice president in charge of research. Also present were the vice president in charge of sales, the chief actuary, the executive vice president and two staff actuaries.

> You say your latest figures show a loss of $68,300 per year for the past three years on policy H-279?

Yes, and it's getting worse this year. Last year we actually put out $75,300 more on that line of policies than we took in.

Joe, we can't go on like this. I know your boys like this policy because it is a good seller, but we're in business to make a profit.

All of the above are typical discussion situations. Each kind of discussion represented here is going on in hundreds of places across the country right now. And these are only a few of the situations and groups from which discussions emerge. Of all types of sustained direct oral communication, none is more common or important to our way of life than discussion. Yet when we study or talk about speech, we are often inclined to focus on the more glamorous but far less frequent process of public speaking — one person doing most of the talking with many persons more or less listening. It is in the process of *shared* talking and listening by two or more people that most of our communication through the spoken word is achieved. Discussion, a give-and-take process, is the medium and the context for the cooperative effort which makes group life of any sort possible. The only alternative to discussion is absolute control by one person. Indeed, discussion emerges almost every time people with a common interest come together.

DISCUSSION: A DEFINITION

A large number of writers have defined discussion in various ways. For the sake of clarity, *discussion* in this book refers to *two or more people talking with one another in order to achieve a mutually satisfactory understanding or solution to a problem.* This seemingly simple definition implies several characteristics of group discussion:

1. *Cooperation is paramount to discussion.* There may be disagreement and argument during a discussion, but all members of a discussion group must cooperate in the search for a group product that will be as satisfactory as possible to all. Argument should become a way of testing the soundness of ideas, rather than a way of winning.
2. *Interaction occurs continuously.* Interaction is defined as "mutual or reciprocal influence between two or more systems," indicating that each member is influencing each other member and in turn is being influenced by each other member.[1] The members are constantly reacting, adapting and modifying their behavior in response to each

---

[1]Horace B. and Ava C. English, *A Comprehensive Dictionary of Psychological and Psychoanalytical Terms* (New York: Longmans, Green and Company, 1958), p. 270.

other. No one can engage in discussion with prepared speeches. Nor can he leave the discussion unchanged by the interaction.

3. *A group exists,* rather than a simple collection of people. The most commonly mentioned characteristic of a group is members with interdependent objectives. Each member has some feeling of need which he hopes to satisfy wholly or in part through discussion. In addition, any group has some shared values and norms.[2]

4. *Speech is the primary medium of communication.* Words and vocal characteristics are the major means by which members interact, although they will also interact through gestures, touch and writing.

5. *Interpersonal perception.* All the above characteristics indicate that members must to some degree be aware of the presence, actions and reactions of each other. A frequently cited definition of *small group* is that "each member receives some impression or perception of each other member distinct enough so that he can . . . give some reaction to each of the others as individual persons, even though it be only to recall that the other was present."[3]

Each of these characteristics will be elaborated on in subsequent chapters.

DISCUSSION AND THE DEMOCRATIC IDEAL

Discussion and democratic process are like the two faces of a coin. Democracy can function only with discussion, and the democratic ideal is *sine qua non* for discussion. The democratic ideal is usually expressed: "All persons affected by a decision shall have some voice in making the decision." Discussion is only a part of the democratic process, but nothing is more essential to it. For example, the bulk of decision-making by Congress is done in committee sessions. A few close decisions may be made in open session with an occasional vote changed by public speeches, but most of the thinking, investigating, compromising, creating, and deciding which result in laws are done in conferences and discussions. So it is in any organization which is relatively democratic.

Autocracy and tyranny are not associated with discussion. Although the tyrant (whether in government, home or business) may consult before making up his mind, he makes the decisions — they are not products of discussion. Indeed, suppression of all public discussion

---

[2]Clovis R. Shepherd, *Small Groups* (San Francisco: Chandler Publishing Company, 1964), p. 5.
[3]Robert F. Bales, *Interaction Process Analysis* (Reading, Mass.: Addison-Wesley Publishing Company, Inc., 1950), p. 33.

concerning alternatives to government policy has occurred and is occuring in such nations as Russia, China, Cuba, and Germany.

Most businessmen today realize that they manage men, not machines, and that men are more creative and productive when they have something to say about how they work. This realization has resulted in a great deal more consultation and discussion in the business world.

America is known as a nation of joiners. Most of us belong to many organizations during our lifetime. Church groups, neighborhood improvement groups, civic organizations, youth groups and study groups all use discussion to make plans and carry out projects.

As the amount of family interaction is reduced by work, school and other activities centered outside the home, the quality of family relationships becomes a matter of serious concern. One outcome is an emphasis on family conversation and discussion. Everyone old enough to understand is likely to have some voice in planning such family matters as recreation and vacations, schooling and major purchases.

Much effort is now being bent toward revitalizing our cities and improving the skills of the less fortunate. One aspect of this work is the need for leadership in community planning. Finding people who know how to work democratically in a discussion format is a major problem. Where skills and attitudes of discussion are nonexistant, they must be developed or the result is apathy, lack of progress and unacceptable solutions.

In short, democratic ideals and procedures depend on discussion, and discussion leads to further growth of democracy. All types of oral communication are important in our world, but the informal give-and-take of discussion is the most vital to a free society. To further clarify the nature and function of this important type of speaking and listening, it will next be compared to other types of speech.

DISCUSSION AND OTHER FORMS OF SPEECH

All forms of communicative speaking have some things in common. Doubtless you have already been introduced to a communication model, explaining in diagrammatic form the process by which perceptions and intentions are encoded, transmitted, received and decoded. All face-to-face oral communication is effected through the medium of light and sound waves using verbal, vocal and gestural symbols. In various types of speech these three kinds of symbols will vary in importance, but all three play a part. Of course, no communication occurs unless someone acts and someone else reacts; oral *communication* always entails both speaking and listening. Little else can be found that is common to all types of speaking. The balance between speaking and listening, the direction of speaking, attitudes, purpose and interpersonal relations — are all notably different among different kinds of speech events.

Balance and Direction of Speaking and Listening

Discussion and other types of group speaking such as conversation and interviewing require that each participant have an equal responsibility to speak and listen. This is not to say all members of a group will speak and listen in equal amounts, but all are equally *responsible* for both speaking and listening. The primary source of communicative acts in a discussion will constantly change, with other participants being secondary sources for the moment. Each person will be primarily a listener, then primarily a speaker, once more a listener and so on.

Public speaking differs from discussion in that the primary source of communicative acts, the speaker, is constant throughout. Some modification occurs in a forum period, but this is usually classified as a form of discussion. Lecture-discussion, the situation where a professor speaks with limited comments and questions from students, is a hybridization of public speaking and discussion.

A very important facet of discussion, one which distinguishes it from all other types of speech, is that the speaker can be called on instantly to account for what he has said. A breach of honesty, a substitution of selfish ends for group good, a violation of the rules of evidence or faulty reasoning can be challenged instantly. Responsibility for doing so rests with all members of the group.

Attitude Differences: Discussion vs. Debate or Persuasion

Dialectic, the search for truth (in the sense of the best possible answer), since the time of Aristotle has been considered to be a counterpart of rhetoric (the science and art of influencing others through speech or writing). Discussion, in most instances, is a form of group dialectic. People who have made up their minds cannot honestly engage in a decision-making or problem-solving discussion. They can only seek to persuade others of the rightness of their prior positions by practicing persuasion, but not by engaging in dialectic. Even learning discussions are stopped by out-and-out debating or persuading; the intent of discussants must be to share, to explore differing conceptions and to foster mutual understanding without trying to win adherents. In this regard, debate and persuasion are diametrically opposed to discussion. If one does not have the ability to tolerate differing opinions he cannot engage in learning discussions and if he has reached unalterable conclusions he cannot engage in decision-making discussions. To pretend to do so is unethical, for it demands from others what one is not willing to do himself — change position. Such a participant will either subvert other participants, stymie group progress or be excluded from the group after much friction and loss of time. To join a group discussion with one's mind made up on the issue facing the group, unable to suspend judgment or to entertain differing points of view is no less than a breach of morality.

Skills in Discussion and Public Address

There appears to be no necessary relationship between skill in public speaking and effectiveness in discussing. You have probably observed that some of your instructors who are excellent lecturers are very poor at stimulating or leading class discussion. The opposite also occurs: the author remembers a professor who was wonderful at conducting a seminar discussion with stimulating questions, guidance, clarification of student comments, and enlightening remarks of his own. As a lecturer, he was a failure; he rambled, spoke to himself, frequently ran out of content before the end of the class period, and so hemmed and hawed that it was often a struggle to stay awake. Thomas Jefferson and George Washington are reputed to have been excellent in informal discussion, but neither made much of a mark as a public speaker. Lincoln and Kennedy, on the other hand, were men of great repute in both conference and public speaking.

The reason is simple: Some of the skills essential to each type of speaking are very different. The detailed skills in organizing a speech are not needed for the short remarks of discussion. Strategy and persuasive devices of use to public speakers may be a serious detriment to developing the trust needed in a discussion group. For example, an associate of the author was once damned by a laboratory training group for being too persuasive and subverting the ideas of others with persuasive techniques. A change was called for, was made, and his status and influence rose rapidly in the group. Direct, forceful delivery may or may not be helpful in discussion, depending on the norms of the group. The very energetic person may be seen as someone to resist. To be skilled in public speaking is not necessarily to be skilled in discussing and vice versa. Appropriate and effective behavior depends on an understanding of differing circumstances. To help you develop such an understanding, the next section of this chapter concerns different types of groups and discussions.

TYPES OF DISCUSSIONS

Discussions can be classified along a number of dimensions. In order to accurately describe a given discussion, one must classify it into at least two dichotomies: public or private and problem-solving or enlightenment. In each of these dichotomies there are several types of discussions. It is important for you to establish an image of the general characteristics of each major type of discussion so that you can communicate about discussions with your classmates and instructor.

Public or Private

Any discussion which takes place for the enlightenment of a listening audience is classified as a public discussion. One which takes place for the sake of the discussants, whether to learn or in order to reach a decision, is called private. Occasionally interested nonparticipants may observe a private discussion (as in the case of a typical city council meeting). It can readily be seen that all problem-solving discussions can be classified as private, whereas learning discussions can be either private or public.

Private Discussion Groups

Small groups (usually 2 to 20 people) exist for many purposes and have their origins in many sources. The student of discussion needs a simplified way of thinking about small group that will help him observe, talk about and analyze the groups with which he will come into contact. The classification scheme provided here is practically rather than theoretically oriented.

Primary or psyche groups These are people who have come together primarily to be with one another rather than to accomplish some task. Examples are the family, the gang which shares fellowship and cokes in the student center, four girls who eat lunch and often attend movies together, friends who take their coffee breaks together or college professors who frequently drop into each other's offices for a chat. Such groups may take on a task from time to time, but more often they discuss to "let off steam," chat about a variety of topics and generally to enjoy each other's company. Their talk is likely to be considerably disorganized, unplanned and highly informal.

Therapy and training groups These are groups of people who have come together to study group interaction, to learn to get along better with others or to overcome personality problems. Members of such groups do not choose each other, but are usually put together by some outside authority like a trainer or therapist. No group product is sought; each individual is seeking personal gain that requires the presence and help of other people who are also seeking to grow as individuals. Such groups are highly artificial, usually have a strong central authority figure (who may appear to be very passive) and have a limited existence. You may find them in a mental hospital, a college leadership laboratory, a prison, a psychiatrist's office, an industry training center, or almost anywhere training and counselling take place. At times your speech class may become this sort of group. It was formed in much the same way as a training group: Several people with a common need were put together under the control of an authority figure, or expert.

Study or learning groups These groups are similar to training and therapy groups. They are formed as a medium for the growth of the participants. However, rather than seeking growth in personality, the members of a learning group seek to understand a subject more thoroughly by pooling their knowledge and different points of view. While they are exchanging knowledge, the participants also get practice in speaking, critical thinking, listening and other skills.

Committees These are groups of people who have been given an assignment by a parent organization or some person in authority. A committee may be formed to investigate and report findings, to recommend a course of action for the parent group, to formulate policies or to plan and carry out some action. All such tasks require discussion among the members. Boards, councils and staffs are special types of committees. For example, the board of directors is often called an executive committee. Such groups represent a larger organization, often with very extensive power to make and execute decisions.

Conference This is a group of representatives taken from different groups. The conferees communicate information from one group to another, or they attempt to work out a solution satisfactory to all groups represented. For example, representatives of various charitable organizations meet to coordinate the efforts of their respective groups or to exchange information and ideas. Representatives of labor and management meet frequently to decide on such matters as wages, working conditions and fringe benefits. A conference group from the House of Representatives and the Senate attempt to settle differences in bills which have been passed in their respective legislative chambers.

The term *conference* is used in many other ways. Sometimes it is used as a synonym for private discussion or interviewing. At other times it is used to refer to a large gathering of persons who will hear speeches, study various topics, and perhaps engage in small group discussions.

In this book, however, it will refer to a meeting of representatives from two or more organizations concerned with similar (or the same) problems.

Public Discussion Groups

Panel is the name of a type of public discussion in which several participants, usually guided by a designated moderator, discuss a topic or problem for the enlightenment of a listening audience. The discussants speak impromptu, interacting directly with each other. A panel usually consists of experts with somewhat different points of view or specialities who have agreed to express informally their knowledge and beliefs for the benefit of an audience.

A *public interview* may be conducted by one or more interviewers, and more than one person may be interviewed at a time. "Meet the Press" is a well-known interview program aired on both radio and television. Interviewers and interviewees usually agree in advance on a list of major questions or topics to be discussed. The interviewers represent the audience by asking questions of the interviewees.

A *symposium* consists of a series of brief public speeches on a single major problem or topic. Although some writers classify symposium as a form of discussion, there is no direct interaction among the speakers. Hence it is not a small-group discussion, and will not be considered further in this book.

Forum refers most often to a period of time when the audience to a panel discussion, lecture, film or other presentation is invited to ask questions or make comments. It is also used to refer to a discussion held by a large gathering of people, such as a hearing on a proposed change in zoning laws or a public hall meeting in which the mayor of a city goes before all interested people to discuss with them any problem concerning city government.

Problem Solving or Enlightenment

The end result sought by a discussion group is either a solution to a problem or individual enlightenment. *Problem solving* and *decision making* can be considered synonyms for most purposes, for in both cases a group decision must be made. An enlightenment (or learning) group may talk about problems and make pseudo decisions, but such a group has no authority to implement or to enforce its decisions. To illustrate, any group of citizens can discuss United States foreign aid policies. They may even reach an agreement, but still they are classified as an enlightenment group for they cannot implement their decisions. If one of these groups decided to write a letter of recommendation to the United States Department of State it would then become a problem-solving group, the problem being "What shall we write in our letter?"

The *advisory* group is a special type of problem-solving group. Such a group lacks the authority to make a binding decision, yet it must produce a decision and plan of action to recommend to some person or organization which has the authority to make the final decision and act on it.

In summary, any discussion which is to result in a group product should be classified as a problem-solving discussion, and any discussion which is to result only in individual learnings should be classified as an enlightenment discussion.

Many other words have been used to refer to variations in discussion formats and groups. We could talk about colloquies, committee hearings, workshops and so forth. However, all of these are modifications of types of discussion already described. The important dimensions for describing any group discussion are the primary purpose of the group, whether or not the meeting is for the sake of the participants or an audience, and when the group is discussing a problem, whether or not it has power to decide or only to advise. The essence of all discussion is a group of people with an interdependent purpose to be achieved (at least in part) by direct and cooperative verbal interaction.

Chapter 2

AN ORIENTATION
TO GROUPS

No doubt you have been puzzled about why some groups are very successful and others fail miserably. You leave one discussion group feeling very satisfied, and then leave another feeling equally frustrated. In one discussion you may be pleased with the fine job you did; you may be quite disappointed with your participation in the next discussion.

If one is to be an effective discussant, he must have a general schema for analyzing and criteria for evaluating any group of which he may be a member. The purpose of this chapter is to help you learn to detect what is needed in group discussions in order to make your own participation both helpful to a group and satisfying to you. If you can analyze accurately, then your behavior can be the result not only of personal inclination but also of the needs of the group. The chapter begins with a clarification of the term *group*, then considers the major dimensions of a group, and finally discusses the attitudes and actions which make an effective group discussant.

GROUP AND "GROUPNESS"

In defining group discussion, it was necessary to mention many of the major characteristics of groups. Now it is time to define and describe the dynamic interpersonal structure which in this book is referred to as a *group*.

The word *group* has been used to refer to many kinds of phenomena: a collection of items (such as trees or numbers); a large organization such as an insurance company, the people who voted for Nixon in 1960, or the members of a religious organization; two or more people having anything in common (such as standing at the same corner while waiting for a bus). In the phrase *group discussion*, we will use the term *group* in a much more restricted sense, it will refer to a specific and definite set of characteristics.

A discussion group has the following characteristics:
1. A number of people sufficiently small for each to be aware of and have some reaction to each other (from 2 to rarely more than 20).
2. A mutually interdependent purpose in which the success of each is contingent upon the success of the others in achieving this goal.
3. Each person has a sense of belonging or membership, identifying himself with the other members of the group.
4. Oral interaction (not all of the interaction will be oral, but a significant characteristic of a discussion group is reciprocal influence exercised by talking).
5. Behavior based on norms and procedures accepted by all members.

Group, in this sense, refers to what is often called a "pattern property," or nonadditive dimension. "Groupness" emerges from the relationships among the people involved, just as "cubeness" emerges from the image of a set of planes, intersects and angles in specific relationships to each other. One can draw a cube with twelve lines (try it), but only if they are assembled in a definite way. Any other arrangement of the lines gives something other than a cube. Likewise, one can have a collection or set of people without having a group or a discussion group. A robber and three policemen may interact orally, but they do not constitute a group (lacking an interdependent purpose, shared norms and procedures). Bridge players may or may not constitute a group, depending on whether or not they have as primary the promotively interdependent purpose of entertainment and enjoying each other's company. A "promotively interdependent purpose" exists when all members succeed or fail together. The success of each is dependent upon the success of all. Each member promotes the success of the others.

In order to understand a discussion group of which one is a member, one must look at many dimensions of the group. We will consider these dimensions in detail. When analyzing a project group in your class, a committee, or any other discussion group you will need to consider these dimensions.

PURPOSE AND SOURCE

What is the promotively interdependent purpose of the group and is it clearly understood by all members? Frequently, group members do not understand why they have been selected for membership in a committee or the purposes of a group they have joined voluntarily. The writer has frequently asked each member of a discussion group to write down the purpose of the discussion and the problem on which the group is working, only to find that every person had a decidedly different idea about the group purpose and problem. In such a situation, no progress can be made since there is no common goal to work toward.

Is the group goal of major importance to all members of the group? Only those people who place a high value on the purpose of the group are likely to work diligently and prepare and contribute significantly.

Is the group professedly established for one purpose, but working toward another? Many continuing groups (such as standing committees) have lost their original reason for being, yet go on interacting aimlessly or toward some vague aim. Such lack of purpose results in inefficiency, dissatisfaction, membership loss and decay of the group.

Confusion of group purpose may also result from hidden agendas. This refers to an objective of an individual member (or a subgroup of members) which is different from the avowed group purpose. For example, one member may be seeking attention in order to get elected to an office. Another may need much response and affection, and may find ways to get it at the expense of the group as a whole. Hidden agendas may or may not be at variance with the group purpose, but we must be on watch for evidence of them in behaviors which are detrimental to the group purpose. If detected, harmful hidden agendas can usually be dealt with by bringing them to the attention of the group.

Confusion can also result when members are uncertain about the kind of end product which they are expected to produce or the limits within which they must operate. Is this a group (such as an advisory committee or staff) which will produce a suggestion for a larger parent organization or an administrator? Is it a group which can only discuss and learn, having no authority to take action? Is it a group seeking only to understand a variety of points of view on a given topic? Limits may be placed on the discussion group by an administrator, by a sponsoring agency, or perhaps by consensus of the members. *Area of freedom* refers to the amount of power the group has to act. If the area of freedom (and concomitant limits) is not clear and kept constantly in mind, trouble is inevitable and the group will be inefficient. The author has seen members of a religious study-discussion group try to convert other members, while the express group purpose was to understand the similarities and differences among religions. These proselyting members were highly unpopular and a definite handicap to the group, for they were trying to accomplish something outside the area of freedom.

Often a discussant can render great service to his group by in-
quiring about the group purpose, whether or not the other members
understand that purpose and feel it is worthwhile. If the answer is unclear or negative, action can be taken to change, clarify or terminate
group activity. If members are dissatisfied with their group, either the
group purpose, individual purpose or group membership (perhaps *en
toto*) should be changed. People working on what they feel is insig-
nificant or against their individual objectives work poorly at best.

STRUCTURE OF POSITIONS, ROLES AND COMMUNICATION

The term *structure* is used here to refer to a complex of ordered
and interrelated parts, forming some perceived whole or object. A group
(the whole) consists of people (parts) who are related to one another
in many ways (complex order, interrelationships). Each person in a
discussion group holds a definite position in relation to each other
person. This position, however, will be related to the purposes of the
group and the work the member is able to do toward achieving group
purposes. For example, the position of a skilled woodworker would be
very different in a group organized to design and build a cabin from
his position in a group planning a boys' club to combat juvenile de-
linquency.

Some discussion groups have certain appointed or elected posts. For
example, most committees have a designated chairman who is responsible
for such duties as calling meetings, planning agendas, coordinating the
work of other committee members and making reports to the parent
organization. A committee may also have a designated secretary or recorder. Study-discussion groups invariably have a designated leader
(or leaders) responsible for initiating and organizing the discussions;
such groups may also have a hostess who supplies light refreshments.
A board of directors will usually consist of the president, the treasurer,
the secretary and other officers of the parent organization, each of
whom has certain definite functions to perform for the board as well
as for the parent body.

Roles

Members of a discussion group may be observed performing a
variety of functions, some helpful, others not helpful. A given discussant
may perform several types of functions, depending on the needs of
the group, his awareness of those needs and his ability to fulfill the
needs. Such functioning has often been called role taking. Many different

classifications of roles have been produced by writers, but one of the oldest remains highly useful for guiding our observations of a discussion group.[1] This set of roles is divided into three broad sets: (1) group task roles, which are behaviors that help the group solve its problem or accomplish its task; (2) group building and maintenance roles, which are behaviors that help members function together as a group and maintain constructive interpersonal relations while doing so; (3) self-centered roles, which are behaviors that can serve only individual aims, often at the expense of the group. When discussing, we should strive to take only constructive roles (task and maintenance), especially those needed at the moment. Theoretically, any role might be taken by any group member, but discussants tend to become specialists by performing certain functions frequently and rarely performing others.

Group Task Roles

These behaviors supply the information, ideas and energy necessary for the group to accomplish its job.

1. *Initiator* — proposes new ideas, new goals, procedures, methods, solutions
2. *Information seeker* — asks for facts, clarification or information from other members, or suggests information is needed before making decisions
3. *Information giver* — offers facts and information, personal experiences and evidence (note that information is useful to accomplishing the task only when it is both pertinent and valid)
4. *Opinion seeker* — draws out convictions and opinions of others, asks for clarification of position or values involved
5. *Opinion giver* — states own belief or opinion, expresses a judgment
6. *Clarifier* — elaborates on idea expressed by another, often by giving an example, illustration or explanation
7. *Coordinator* — clarifies relationships among facts, ideas and suggestions, or suggests an integration of ideas and activities of two or more members
8. *Orienter* — clarifies purpose or goal, defines position of the group, summarizes or suggests the direction of the discussion
9. *Energizer* — prods group to greater activity or to a decision, stimulates activity, or warns of need to act while still time

---

[1]Kenneth D. Benne and Paul Sheats, "Functional Roles of Group Members," *Journal of Social Issues* 4 (1948), pp. 41-49.

10. *Procedure developer* — offers suggestions for accomplishing ideas of others, or handles such tasks as seating arrangements, running the projector, passing out papers and so forth
11. *Recorder* — keeps written record on paper, chart or blackboard, serving as group's "memory"

Group Building and Maintenance Roles

These behaviors establish and maintain cooperative interpersonal relationships and a group-centered orientation.

1. *Supporter* — praises, agrees, indicates warmth and solidarity with others or goes along with them
2. *Harmonizer* — mediates differences between others, reconciles disagreement, conciliates
3. *Tension reliever* — jokes or brings out humor in a situation, reduces formality and status differences, relaxes others
4. *Gatekeeper* — opens channels of communication, brings in members who otherwise might not speak, sees that all have equitable chance to be heard

Self-Centered Roles

These are behaviors which can only satisfy individual needs and which do not serve the group; most of them are harmful to group maintenance and a detriment to accomplishing the group task. Listed are only a few of the more common self-centered roles.

1. *Blocker* — constantly raises objections, insists nothing can be done, or repeatedly brings up the same topic after the rest of the group has disposed of it
2. *Aggressor* — deflates status of others, expresses disapproval, jokes at expense of another member, expresses ill will or envy
3. *Recognition seeker* — boasts, calls attention to self, relates irrelevant personal experiences, seeks sympathy or pity
4. *Confessor* — uses group as audience for his mistakes, feelings and beliefs irrelevant to the group task or engages in personal catharsis
5. *Playboy* — displays a lack of involvement in group task by making jokes and cynical comments and through horseplay and ridicule
6. *Dominator* — tries to run the group by giving directions, ordering, flattering, interrupting and insisting on his own way
7. *Special-interest pleader* — speaks up primarily for the interests of a different group, acting as its representative, apologist, or advocate

Communication Networks

Not only will discussants develop specialized roles in a group; they will also develop a definite network of communication within the group. A member who begins a meeting may find others wanting him to initiate the discussion at subsequent meetings. A person who monopolizes the expression of opinions will find others turning to him for his reaction after each new idea is proposed. An infrequent speaker will find that others tend to overlook him, and that it is increasingly difficult for him to get into the conversation.

The type of communication network has great effects on the discussion group. Some networks are desirable; others are downright harmful to productivity, the satisfaction of members, and group maintenance. A leader-centered network can sometimes speed up decision making, but it may exclude vital information held by a reticent member and a lower morale. The network may exclude some members, leading to subdivisions and group disintegration. Four types of frequently observed communication networks, along with implications of each, are described in the following section. It is important to realize that any of these patterns may exist for a brief time in any discussion group. The general or typical network is what matters.

1. The *wheel,* or *recitative pattern* is so called because almost all talking is directed to one member. This is the pattern in a recitation class where the teacher asks a question of a pupil who replies to the teacher, then the teacher replies to that pupil or speaks directly to another and so on. A dominating discussion leader will produce this pattern by insisting that all persons be recognized by him before they speak, by restating comments, asking all questions and generally controlling all participation. A desirable variant of this pattern may emerge for a short time when one member has special information or when the group tries to bring a deviant member to agree with the rest of the group. While this pattern may be very efficient since many solutions can be obtained in a minimum amount of time, it tends to reduce innovation, breed dependency on the leader and lower group cohesiveness.

2. Somtimes a two or three level *hierarchial network* of interaction emerges in a discussion group. In one form of subgrouping, two or more relatively low-power members interact with a higher power member, but not with each other. The high-power members interact with each other, but not with the members of each other's subgroups. If there is a third level of power, the "lieutenants" will not interact much with each other, but will interact with their subordinates and the top

man or central leader. Such a pattern of communication indicates a serious split in the group, with subgroup goals taking priority over the common goal.

3. A more common form of subgrouping involves the two or more *private conversations* which take place within the context of the larger group. Such conversations take some members out of the discussion and weaken the pool of information and ideas available to the whole group. Such subgrouping occurs when there is too much individual desire to participate in the topic, when discussion is not on a topic of interest to some members, or when a subgroup has split from the main group. Feelings and interest may be so high that some members will not wait to get into the group conversation. Boredom may lead them to talk with neighbors about some more interesting topic, such as dating or family problems. Occasional brief subgrouping of this sort is not a serious enough problem to warrant action, but if persistent, it must be stopped. The designated leader or observer should ask why it is occurring. Is the group off the track? Is there too little opportunity for some members to participate? Is the group pursuing unacceptable or irrelevant goals? In any case, the problem should be pointed out and the group should talk about it openly in order to determine the cause and decide what to do about it.

4. For the small discussion group, the *all-channel network* is most desirable. It permits rapid communication without getting clearance from a central authority. Everyone is free to speak up and say what he has to say while it is still pertinent and fresh in mind. Communication flows freely from one person to another, according to whoever is moved to speak at the moment. Attention will shift frequently and quite at random from person to person. Most of the comments will be directed to the group as a whole, rather than to individual members. Such group-centered comments tend to keep the channels of communication open to everyone, encouraging any and all to speak, and permitting free feedback of questions and answers among members. Many studies have shown morale to be highest in an all-channel network.[2] Departures from this pattern should be relatively brief.

NORMS

Every group develops *norms*. These are expectations of how members should behave, rules of conduct or standards for participation.

---

[2]For example, see Harold J. Leavitt and Ronald A. Mueller, "Some Effects of Feedback on Communication," in A. Paul Hare, Edgar F. Borgatta, and Robert F. Bales (eds.), *Small Groups* (New York: Alfred A. Knopf, Inc., 1955), p. 423.

Norms reflect and determine how one speaks, to whom he speaks, how he dresses, where and how he sits, what he talks about, what his activities are, what sentiments he expresses, how he expresses them, and so forth. Such norms may or may not be stated, but they can be detected by an observer on the basis of behavior in the group. Conformity to procedural norms is essential if members are to work together. Discussants are usually inclined to conform to the procedural norms of the group.[3] Any violation of the norms may mean the norm is not understood by the violator or he disagrees with it. If procedural norms are clearly understood but still violated by one or more members, this should be called to the attention of the group and some action should be taken. Continued violation means the member feels the norm is somehow detrimental.

The degree to which a member will conform to group norms (both procedural and opinion norms) depends on his evaluation of the group and his status in it. The more a person prizes membership in a group, the more he will conform; the higher his status, the more he will conform.[4]

In order to clarify and possibly change the norms of a discussion group, first study their effects. Group awareness of harmful effects can lead to change. A participant should try to discover answers to the following questions:

1. What regularities of behavior can be seen? (For example, who talks to whom? How do the people talk? Where do they sit? To what degree do they ask for evidence supporting a position? How are ideas evaluated?)
2. What seem to be the practical effects of each of these modes of behaving? (For example, are ideas going untested? Are some members' ideas accepted uncritically while others' ideas are ignored or rejected? Do members always sit in the same positions? Is there much evidence of frustration?)
3. What happens when a member deviates from a norm?

GROUP SIZE

The number of persons forming a group is a major determinant of what happens during discussions. A person needs to be flexible in ad-

---

[3]Do not confuse conformity in procedure with conformity in thinking. While conformity in procedure is necessary, unthinking conformity to majority opinion can be very damaging both to group products and to individual personality.

[4]For a simple explanation of how certain norms affect participation, see Clovis R. Shepherd, *Small Groups* (San Francisco: Chandler Publishing Company, 1964), pp. 41, 77-94.

justing to groups of different sizes. As group size increases, the complexity increases rapidly; the number of interpersonal relationships increases geometrically as the number of members increases arithmetically. Thus a group of two people has one interpersonal relationship; a group of three people has three; a group of five people has ten; a group of ten people has forty-five; a group of twenty people has 190 relationships.

Increased size means less opportunity for the average participant to speak and to influence others. In student learning groups, increased size results in lower satisfaction with the discussion.[5] Frustration increases with group size. In larger groups, the less forceful and confident discussants speak less, while the more forceful tend to occupy an even greater proportion of the time. There is a tendency for one central person to do a proportionately greater amount of talking.[6] Also, speeches tend to be longer, often including several points not particularly pertinent to the issue of the moment.

As group size increases, more centralized control of procedures is both expected and needed. Leadership roles become more specialized and formal. Great demands are made on designated leaders to keep order, to keep the discussion organized, and to control the flow of communication.

Other effects commonly occurring when group size increases include greater difficulty in establishing criteria or values, more time reaching a decision, lowering of cohesiveness (attraction to the group), and a tendency for cliques to develop within the group.[7] Small wonder, then, that students who have become proficient in discussing in groups of five to seven often flounder in confusion when the class as a whole tries to engage in discussion with the same sort of informality and loose structure used in the smaller groups.

How large should a discussion group be? The answer depends on the task and purpose of the group. For committees and other problem-solving groups, the ideal size seems to be about five, which is small enough to permit informality and ease in reaching decisions, yet large enough to bring the many types of information and varied points of view needed for wise decisions. For learning groups, the answer may range from as few as three to as many as twenty. If the purpose is to encourage individual questioning and thinking, choose a small group.

---

[5]James A. Schellenberg, "Group Size as a Factor in Success of Academic Discussion Groups," *Journal of Educational Psychology* 33 (1959), pp. 73-79.

[6]E. F. Stephan and E. G. Mishler, "The Distribution of Participation in Small Groups," *American Sociological Review* 17 (1952), pp. 598-608.

[7]See bibliography for research sources which support these generalizations.

If the purpose is to expose participants to as many points of view as possible, a larger group is better.

In this chapter the concept of group discussion and the major variables which affect group discussion have been considered. The importance of understanding the group concept, and the effects of group purpose, origin, positions, roles, communication networks, norms and size cannot be overestimated. In some cases, many other factors may have to be considered. Detailed consideration has been given to these factors in recent books on small-group psychology. From this chapter you should have developed the kind of analytical framework needed to plan and adapt to conditions in small discussion groups.

BIBLIOGRAPHY

Benne, Kenneth D., and Sheats, Paul, "Functional Roles of Group Members," *Journal of Social Issues* 4, 1948, pp. 41-49.

Braden, Waldo W., and Brandenburg, Earnest, *Oral Decision-Making*, New York: Harper and Brothers, 1955, ch. XIII.

Collins, Barry E., and Guetzkow, Harold, *A Social Psychology of Group Processes for Decision-Making*, New York: John Wiley & Sons, Inc., 1964.

Golembiewski, Robert T., *The Small Group: An Analysis of Research Concepts and Operations*, Chicago: The University of Chicago Press, 1962.

Hare, A. Paul, *Handbook of Small Group Research*, New York: The Free Press of Glencoe, 1962.

Hare, A. Paul, Borgatta, Edgar F., and Bales, Robert F., (eds.), *Small Groups*, New York: Alfred A. Knopf, Inc., 1955.

Harnack, R. Victor, and Fest, Thorrel B., *Group Discussion: Theory and Technique*, New York: Appleton-Century-Crofts, 1964.

Homans, George C., *The Human Group*, New York: Harcourt, Brace and Company, 1950.

Shepherd, Clovis R., *Small Groups*, San Francisco: Chandler Publishing Company, 1964.

Chapter 3

ORGANIZING GROUP DISCUSSION

Many of us are so used to discussing anything, anywhere, anytime that planning and following a pattern or outline for discussion may seem unnecessary. After all, we've discussed problems, made decisions, and taken action as members of groups. Yet the most common complaint by participants in adult discussion groups observed by the author was that leaders failed to keep the group on the track and the discussion organized.

Have you noticed how easy it is to overlook some important fact when you tackle a problem alone? Do you find your thoughts often coming in a random, jumbled, helter-skelter fashion? Have you re-gretted decisions made before all the needed evidence was considered or possible alternatives explored? If individual thinking is often hap-hazard, consider what can happen when a group of people try to think together toward a common aim. Each person may have a different way of approaching the subject or problem. If each follows his own lead, there will not be a group discussion, but individuals talking to themselves. Perhaps you have noticed how often conversation is shallow and vacuous, shifting aimlessly from topic to topic, with no one getting his feelings and meanings clearly expressed about anything. If so, you are aware of the need for some pattern or plan for talking if discussion is to be meaningful. Let's consider a couple of examples, both observed in adult study-discussion groups.

Ten persons were responding to each other's comments about a set of readings on "Status and Role." In one swoop they went from an exploration of conflicting roles of a contemporary African leader to one discussant's troubles with a trucking union. Next they jumped to unions in general, then to contemporary literary magazines — all in the span of five minutes. They never did get back to the readings.

Quite different was a discussion in which eighteen adults were analyzing two of E. E. Cummings' poems. Talk was excited and spontaneous, but the remarks were clearly interrelated. One speaker mentioned the picture he thought the poet wanted to create with a particular line of the poem. A second added a further interpretation. The third speaker explained why he disagreed somewhat, followed by nods and verbal agreement. A fourth speaker gave his views on the next stanza. The designated discussion leader asked if there was anything in the poem to support this interpretation. The prior speaker began to explain, then stopped, and began again with, "Now I see what you mean." On and on went the group in a gradual unfolding of the poem. Finally, one speaker attempted a synthesis of the many varying points expressed. As the discussion closed, the members spoke of how much they had enjoyed it and how much better they now understood and appreciated the poems.

These two brief examples illustrate several differences between disorganized talk and organized group thinking. In the first instance, the talk was scattered among many topics and going nowhere; in the second, the talk was easy to follow, fruitful of understanding, with each comment a natural outgrowth of what had preceded it. In the first case, the discussion sounded like an undisciplined train of free association; in the second, the statements resembled the workings of a trained, controlled mind. This chapter is designed to help you achieve discussions like the second. First, we will examine some of the characteristics of effective group thinking; second, we will look at alternative patterns for organizing group problem solving; third, we will look at means for organizing enlightenment or learning discussions.

GROUP THINKING

As Keltner (and others) has pointed out, thinking in the context of a group is still a process which occurs within the nervous system of each individual, not in the group in some suprapersonal way.[1] But when each member understands and utilizes all that he can of the other member's statements in advancing the group — whether or not one chooses to call this occurrence group thinking — we can say that a sort of *promotively interdependent thinking* has occurred. Most of the statements and subvocal reactions of group members are dovetailed; each is related to, based upon, and to some degree assimilated with what has preceded. The discussion is directed toward the discovery of

---

[1]John Keltner, " 'Groupthink' and Individual Thinking," *Today's Speech* 5, (April, 1957), pp. 5-6.

common ends and of mutually acceptable means to the goals. Minds are attuned like the players in a "jam" session, with each discussant contributing to the total effect, catching his cues from what his fellows are doing, and being guided throughout by a central theme or "melody" which serves to organize and give power.

Such group thinking does not result merely from following rules of logic or some preplanned outline. Procedure need not be projected and controlled by one member (leader). Nor is such thinking by group members necessarily the result of studying discussion techniques. But some shared logic or mode of thinking is essential to it. Training in discussion techniques and procedural controls, and an understanding of the modes of critical thinking will contribute much to intellectual teamwork if other necessary conditions exist. We have already examined some of the preconditions necessary to promote interdependent thinking. Next we will consider some of the patterns for group thinking. The *reflective thinking sequence* or some other pattern more appropriate to the problem or topic is invariably evident in the talk of groups which display a high degree of promotively interdependent thinking. The pattern in such cases is shared rather than imposed on the group.

Consider an analogy of group thinking to traveling. Before starting on a journey, we first develop some idea of the destination even though we may never have been there before. We map out in advance the sequence of routes we will follow, the major cities and landmarks that should be noticed as we proceed from point of origin to goal. We watch for these as we proceed, sometimes making unplanned detours or stops, and correcting our course after every deviation from the planned route. So, too, must be the conduct of those who wish to be effective in the art of discussion. They must have a planned route, watch for major and minor landmarks, make adjustments, and keep a constant check on progress toward the goal.

GROUP PROBLEM SOLVING

General Principles

A limited amount of research has been done on the merits of various patterns for group problem-solving discussion. Maier and Maier found that a "developmental pattern," while taking more patience and skill on the part of the designated leader, produced a better quality of decision than did a simpler problem-solution ("free") pattern.[2] The "develop-

---

[2]N. R. F. Maier and R. A. Maier, "An Experimental Test of the Effects of 'Developmental' vs. 'Free' Discussions on the Quality of Group Decisions," *Journal of Applied Psychology* 41, (1957), pp. 320-323.

mental pattern," somewhat like the creative problem-solving pattern below, breaks the problem into a series of distinct issues and steps. It forces the group to map out the problem thoroughly and systematically. In a "free" discussion, the group discusses the problem and tries to find a solution. In a similar study, Maier and Solem found that a leader technique for delaying the group decision produced solutions to a "change of work procedure" problem superior to those solutions produced when "free" discussion was permitted.[3]

The effects of three different patterns for problem-solving discussion were compared experimentally by Brilhart and Jochem. A creative problem-solving pattern produced more possible solutions, and more solutions judged to be good ideas by independent judges. Participants preferred the creative problem-solving method to the simpler pattern of problem, possible solutions and final solution. Significantly, more subjects also preferred a creative problem-solving pattern in which possible solutions preceded criteria to one in which criteria preceded possible solutions. Several subjects indicated they felt discussing criteria first hampered their freedom to express novel ideas.[4] In a subsequent study (not yet published), Brilhart compared the creative-thinking sequence and the simpler reflective-thinking sequence to see which ideas were evaluated when first mentioned. Those tested in this latter study made binding decisions on problems which affected them personally: how to distribute grade points among themselves, and the date of the final examination in their speech course. Again, significantly more subjects preferred the detailed creative problem-solving pattern.

Parnes and his associates have found that brainstorming techniques, in which no judging or criticism of any type is permitted while ideas are being proposed and listed, produced many more new and good ideas than did ordinary problem-solving procedures. Parnes also recommended establishing detailed criteria only after possible ideas have been listed by the group.[5]

---

[3]N. R. F. Maier and A. R. Solem, "The Contribution of a Discussion Leader to the Quality of Group Thinking: The Effective Use of Minority Opinions," *Human Relations* 5 (1952), pp. 277-288.

[4]John K. Brilhart and Lurene M. Jochem, "Effects of Different Patterns on Outcomes of Problem-Solving Discussion," *Journal of Applied Psychology* 48 (1964), pp. 175-179.

[5]Sidney J. Parnes and Harold F. Harding (eds.), *A Source Book for Creative Thinking* (New York: Charles Scribner's Sons, 1962), pp. 19-30, 185-191, 283-290.

Sidney J. Parnes, "Effects of Extended Effort in Creative Problem-Solving," *Journal of Educational Psychology* 52 (1961), pp. 117-122.

Sidney J. Parnes and Arnold Meadow, "Effects of 'Brainstorming' Instructions on Creative Problem-Solving by Trained and Untrained Subjects," *Journal of Educational Psychology* 50 (1959), pp. 171-176.

From these research findings and other experience with discussions, we can establish some basic principles which apply regardless of the specific pattern outline being followed by the group.

Focus on the Problem before Solutions

What would you think if you drove into a garage with a car that was running poorly and the mechanic almost immediately said, "What you need to fix this buggy is a new carburetor and a set of spark plugs." If your reaction is like mine, you would get out of there as fast as your ailing auto would let you. A competent mechanic after he asked questions about how the car was acting and observed how it ran, would put it on an electronic engine analyzer. After gathering information by these means he would make a tentative diagnosis, which he would check by direct examination of the suspected parts. Only then would he say something like, "The problem is that two of your valves are burned, and the carburetor is so badly worn that it won't stay adjusted properly."

Our two hypothetical mechanics illustrate one of the most common failings in group (and individual) problem solving: solution centeredness. Irving Lee, after observing many problem-solving conferences and discussions, found that in most of the groups he studied there was "a deeply held assumption that because the problem was announced it was understood. People seemed too often to consider a complaint equivalent to a description, a charge the same as a specification."[6] Maier, after many years of studying problem-solving discussions in business and industry, stated that "participants as well as discussion leaders focus on the objective of arriving at a solution and fail to give due consideration to an exploration of the problem."[7] Groups tend to act like a surgeon who scheduled an operation when a patient complained of a pain in his abdomen, like a judge who handed down a decision as soon as he had read the indictment, or like the hunter who shot at a noise in the bushes and killed his son. Solution-centeredness has harmful effects:

1. *Partisanship is encouraged.* Participants spend a lot of time arguing the merits of their pet proposals. The group often becomes hopelessly split, or negative feeling is aroused which will affect future discussions.

---

[6]Irving J. Lee, *How to Talk with People* (New York: Harper and Brothers, 1952), p. 62.
[7]Norman R. F. Maier, *Problem-Solving Discussions and Conferences* (New York: McGraw-Hill Book Company, 1963), p. 123.

2. *Ineffectual solutions tend to be adopted.* There is a tendency to spend much time debating the first and most obvious solutions, which are usually taken bodily from other situations and are not based on the facts of the present case. New, innovative ideas are not considered.

3. *Time is wasted.* Solution-at-once methods often result in a sort of pinwheel pattern. The problem is mentioned; someone proposes a solution which is argued at length; someone points out that an important aspect of the problem has been neglected; someone then goes back to the problem to see if this is so. This problem-solution cycle may be repeated indefinitely, wasting time on solutions which do not fit the facts of the case. At first, focus on what has gone wrong rather than what shall be done about it?

BEGIN WITH A PROBLEM QUESTION RATHER THAN A SOLUTION QUESTION

How the problem is initially presented to a group and phrased as a question is vital to what follows. Begin with a *problem* question rather than a *solution* question. Consider the following situation: A student leader asks his group, "How can we get rid of a club president who is not doing his job, without further disrupting the club?" Such a statement of the problem appears insoluble, like how to eat a cake and have it too. The apparent dilemma is the result of incorporating a solution (get rid of the president) into the statement of the problem. The better procedure is to separate the solution from the problem, then focus on understanding the details of the problem. Once this has been done, appropriate solutions will usually emerge. Our student leader might ask, "How might we get good leadership for our club?" Then the group can dig into what is expected of the president, how the incumbent is acting, what members are complaining about, what is wrong, and why. Answers to these questions about the problem may lead to tentative solutions: "Send him to a leadership training laboratory;" "Have the sponsor instruct him in his duties;" "Ask him to resign;" "Temporarily assign part of his duties to the executive committee members" and the like. See if you can distinguish between the following problems which include solutions (solution questions) and those which focus on what is wrong:

How can I transfer a man who is popular in the work group but slows down the work of others?

What can be done to alleviate complaints about inadequate parking space at our college?

How might we reduce theft and mutilation in the college library?

How can we get more students to enroll in physics?

What action shall we take in the case of Joe Blevins who is accused of cheating on Professor Lamdeau's exam?

MAP THE PROBLEM SITUATION

To help develop problem mindedness, think of the problem as a large uncharted map with only vague boundaries. The first task facing the problem-solving group is to make the map as complete as possible (in other words, to fully diagnose the situation). The leader of the group should urge the members to tell all they know about the situation: facts, complaints, conditions, circumstances, factors, details, happenings, relationships, disturbances, effects. In short, what have you observed? What have others observed? What have you heard?

At best the "map" of the problem will be incomplete, with full detail in some parts, but gaps or faint outlines in others. Members will disagree on some details. Some observations may be spotty and fleeting. Sometimes the members will admit they do not know enough about the problem to deal with it intelligently. The author remembers a group of students concerned with recommending solutions to a severe shortage of parking space at a large university. The discussants soon decided they did not have enough information to make wise recommendations. They tried to list the types of information they would need before proceeding to talk about solutions. Soon investigating teams were out interviewing, getting maps, collecting records and reading. The subsequent discussions led to a clear description of the many problems involved, and ultimately to a set of recommendations with which the entire group was pleased. These recommendations were presented to proper authorities, and most of them put into effect within three years. When a group gets into a discussion of what must be done to get needed information, the spirit of teamwork is something to behold! And the solutions usually work.

Perhaps the greatest obstacle to problem-centered thinking is the leader or other member who comes to the group with the problem solved in his own mind. Needed is the spirit of humility, which does not know too much and realizes all of us know only a part.

Agree Upon Criteria

Many times there is a lack of "reality testing" before a decision is made final. Other times, a group cannot agree on which of two or more possible solutions to adopt. If the problem has been fully explored, the most likely source of difficulty is a lack of clear-cut standards, criteria, or objectives. In many discussions there is a need for two considerations of criteria: first, when formulating the specific objectives of the group; second, when stating specific standards to be used in judging among solutions. Until agreement (explicit or intuitive) is reached on criteria, agreement on a solution is unlikely.

From the beginning of the discussion, the group needs to be clearly aware of the limitations placed upon it. This is sometimes called the group's area of freedom. The group which tries to make decisions affecting matters over which it has no authority will be both confused and frustrated. For example, the area of freedom for a group of university students includes recommending changes in teaching methods, but students have no authority to make or enforce policy governing such changes. A committee may be given power to recommend plans for a new building, but not to make the final decision and contract for the building. Any policy decision or plan of action must be judged by whether or not it fits into the group's area of freedom. Thus, if a committee is authorized to spend up to $500.00, it must evaluate all possible ideas by that absolute criterion.

It is important to rank criteria, giving priority to those which must be met. Ideas proposed can be rated "yes" or "no" on whether they meet all the absolute criteria, and from "excellent" to "poor" on how well they measure up to the less important criteria.

Single words, such as *efficient*, are not criteria, but categories of criteria. Such words are so vague that they are meaningless when applied to possible solutions. They can be used to find specific criteria. Criteria should be worded as questions or absolute statements. For example, the following criteria might be applied to plans for a club's annual banquet:

Absolute — Must not cost over $400.00 for entertainment.
　　　　　Must be enjoyable to both members and their families.

Questions—How convenient is the location for members?
　　　　　How comfortable is the room?

Defer Judgment When Finding Solutions

Instead of evaluating each possible solution when it is first proposed, defer judgment until a complete list of possible solutions has been produced. Much of the research already quoted indicates that the process of *idea getting* should be separated from *idea evaluation*. Judgment stifles unusual and novel ideas. New ideas come from a minority, and do not have the support of experience or common sense. It is a good idea to list the proposed solutions on a chart or chalkboard. Encouragement should be given to combine, modify or build upon previous suggestions. Get as many ideas as you can, and permit no criticism of them until after the list is complete.

Plan How to Implement and Follow-up

Many times a group will arrive to no avail at a policy decision, a solution to a problem, a resolution or some advice. No plans are made for putting it into effect or to see if the ideas are received by the proper authorities. Every problem-solving discussion should terminate in some plan for action; no such group should consider its work finished until agreement is reached on who is to do exactly what, by what time, and how. If a committee is to make recommendations to a parent body, the committee should decide who will make the report, when he will make it, and in what form. If this report is to be made at a membership meeting, the committee members may then decide to prepare seconding or supporting speeches, may decide how to prepare the general membership to accept their recommendations and so forth. A neighborhood group that has decided to turn a vacant lot into a playground would have to plan how to get legal clearances, who to get to do the work, where to get the materials (or at least from whom), and how to check on the use children get from the playground. No good chairman or leader of a problem-solving group would fail to see that the group worked out details of how to put their decisions into effect.

With these general principles for patterning and organizing effective problem-solving discussions, we now turn to specific patterns for guiding a group's thinking and talking. The headings and questions below are suggestive; the wording should be modified to fit the specific problem.

Specific Patterns for Group Problem Solving

The Creative Problem-Solving Sequence

  I. What is the nature of the problem?
    A. What are we talking about? Is the wording of the problem question clear to us?
    B. What is our area of freedom? What limits should we place on our consideration of the problem? Are we to plan and take action, to make a policy decision, or to advise?
    C. What has been happening? What information do we have about the problem? (This is often called the fact-finding phase of discussion.)

1. Who is affected, how, and under what conditions?
2. What seems to have gone wrong? How do we know?
3. What additional information might we need? How might we obtain it?
4. What factors seem to have contributed to the problem?
5. What present or past steps have been taken to remedy the problem, and how did they work?

   D. What exactly is the problem? What is the meaning of all our information? (At this point the group will want to summarize.)

      1. Can we now state the problem clearly in terms of our findings and objectives?

      2. Have we located a set of subproblems which should be tackled one at a time? If so, what are they, and in what order shall we take them up?

 II. What might be done to solve the problem (or first subproblem)? (List *all* ideas which group members invent.)

III. By what specific criteria shall we judge among our possible solutions? (List and rank these by group agreement.)

IV. What are the relative merits of our possible solutions?

   A. What ideas can we screen out as unrelated to the facts of the problem?

   B. Are there any ideas we should not consider further?

   C. Can we combine and simplify in any way?

   D. How well do the remaining ideas measure up to the criteria?

 V. What will be our final solution or recommendation?

   A. Shall we act on one of these ideas, or apply a combination of two or more? (The group may need to discuss the advantages and disadvantages of each remaining idea. Sometimes it is wise to review the details of the problem. Vote *only if unanimous agreement cannot be reached.*)

   B. How will we state our conclusions?

VI. How will we put our solution into effect?

   A. Who will do what, and when?

   B. Do we need any follow-up or check procedures?

The Reflective-Thinking Sequence

This pattern for group problem-solving discussion is based on the model of problem-solving thinking originally proposed by John Dewey, with modifications espoused in numerous textbooks on conference and discussion. Sometimes the listing of possible solutions and the evaluation of them are separated, but often each idea is evaluated when it is first presented.

I. What is the nature of the problem? (Clarify and analyze.)
II. What will we do to solve the problem? (Possible solutions are listed and evaluated.)
III. How will we put our solution into effect?

Some writers have recommended the following model of reflective thinking as a pattern for group problem-solving discussion.

I. Define and limit the problem.
II. Describe, analyze and evaluate the problem.
III. Establish criteria by which solutions may be judged.
IV. Evaluate the probable consequences of each possible solution.
V. Select the preferred final solution.
VI. Plan how to put the solution into effect.[8]

Still other patterns are possible for group problem-solving thinking. The pattern will need to be abbreviated considerably if the group is to recommend a list of possible solutions, investigate and report on a problem, define a policy without proposing how to put it into effect, or put into effect a solution or policy given to it by a higher authority.

The Leader's Outline

A study outline may get very long and involved. The leader gets so involved in trying to follow it that he is unable to listen well and adapt to what is happening in the group. What the leader needs is a short, simple outline based on the pattern for problem solving which the group has decided to use for organizing its thinking and talking. Such an outline, in abbreviated form, can be put on a chart for all to see and follow, or perhaps duplicated and given to each member of the group. Such a visual model was felt to be most helpful by the subjects in one investigation.[9] Study carefully the following example of a leader's outline for guiding a group through the process of creative problem solving on a specific problem. Notice how the general questions from the model outlines above have been worded in terms of the specific prob-

---

[8]For example, see Russell H. Wagner and Carroll C. Arnold, *Handbook of Group Discussion*, 2nd ed., (Boston: Houghton Mifflin Company, 1965), pp. 70-72
[9]John K. Brilhart, "An Experimental Comparison of Three Techniques for Communicating a Problem-Solving Pattern to Members of a Discussion Group," *Speech Monographs* 33 (1966), pp. 168-177.

lem. The leader, in actually using this outline, further revised his questions to fit the group's findings. He kept notes on his copy of the outline, modifying it as the group proceeded.

Problem Question How might theft and mutilation of materials in the university library be reduced to a minimum?

I. What is the nature of the theft and mutilation now occurring in the library?
   A. Is the question clear to all of us?
   B. What limitations must we consider in our discussion?
      1. We can only recommend and advise; we are to draw up a proposal to be offered to the library committee.
      2. Do we want to place any other limits on our discussion of the problem at this time?
   C. What has been happening?
      1. What has been stolen or mutilated?
      2. How extensive and serious is this loss?
      3. What factors seem to contribute to the problem?
         a. In the library
         b. In the classroom
         c. Students and society at large
         d. Other
      4. Have any steps been taken to reduce the loss? If so, how did they work?
   D. Can we summarize our findings and formulate the exact problem which we must try to solve?

II. In view of the findings, what might we do to reduce theft and mutilation of library materials?
   A. Types of materials (books, periodicals, etc.)?
   B. Any rearrangements?
   C. Additional facilities or staff?
   D. Publicity or campaigns?
   E. Other ideas?

III. By what criteria shall we judge the ideas we have listed?
   A. Are there any absolute standards by which to judge them?
   B. What features should a solution have?

IV. How well does each idea measure up to our criteria?
   A. Can we now combine or synthesize any ideas?
   B. Are there any ideas which we can reject at face value?
   C. How does each remaining idea measure up to our criteria?

V. What will we recommend to the senate library committee?

VI. How will we prepare and present the report?

VII. Do we want to check up on what they do about it?

Brainstorming

Occasionally a problem-solving group may want to engage in a full-fledged brainstorming discussion. Brainstorming depends on the deferment of judgment; many auxiliary skills and techniques can be used to advantage. Brainstorming can be applied to any problem if there is a wide range of possible solutions, none of which can in advance be said to be just right. The process of brainstorming can be applied to any phase of the discussion: finding information (What information do we need? How might we get this information?), finding criteria (What criteria might we use to test ideas?), finding ideas (What might we do?), or implementation (How might we put our decision into effect?). In addition to what has been said about creative problem solving, the following rules of brainstorming should be presented to the group:

1. *All criticism is ruled out while brainstorming.*
2. *The wilder the ideas, the better.* Even offbeat, impractical suggestions may suggest practical ideas to other members.
3. *Quantity is wanted.* The more ideas, the more likelihood of good ones.
4. *Combination and improvement are wanted.* If you see a way to improve on a previous idea, snap your fingers to get attention so it can be recorded at once.

It is often advantageous to have in the discussion group both people with experience and people quite new to the specific problem (for a fresh point of view). A full-time recorder is needed to write down ideas as fast as they are suggested. Sometimes this can be done with a tape recorder, but a visual record that all can see is best. Be sure the recorder gets all ideas in accurate form.

The flow of possible solutions can sometimes be increased by asking idea-spurring questions. One can ask: "How can we adapt (modify, rearrange, reverse, combine, minimize, maximize) *any general solution?*" A concrete suggestion can be used to open up creative thinking in a whole area. For example, someone might suggest: "Place a guard at each door." The leader could then ask, "What else might be done to increase security?" When the group seems to have run out of ideas, try reviewing the list rapidly; then ask for a definite number of additional suggestions to see if you can get more ideas. Usually you will get many more, including some very good ones.

A few warnings about applying brainstorming should be mentioned. A thorough job of creating new ideas, based on a full understanding of the problem, takes time. If hurried, use a more conventional and simple pattern. Be sure to stop all criticism, whether stated or implied by voice or manner. Everyone must feel completely free to express any idea that occurs to him as a possible solution. There are a few people who seem to be unable to separate ideation from evaluation. If a few attempts fail to stop a person from criticizing ideas, ask him to follow the rules, stay quiet, or leave the group. The problem must be clear, carefully analyzed, and closely limited and defined. Broad, sweeping problems must be broken down into subproblems. Vague generalities cannot be put into action.

Lists of ideas must be critically screened and tested against criteria before laying plans for action. Status and interpersonal tensions must be reduced to a minimum.

The leader may want a simpler outline that does not lend itself to brainstorming. Here is an example:

I. What sort of written final exam should we have in our discussion class?
   A. How much authority (area of freedom) do we have?
   B. What facts and feelings should we take into account as we seek to answer this question?

II. What are our objectives (criteria) in deciding on the type of exam?
   A. Learning objectives?
   B. Grades?
   C. Type of preparation and study?
   D. Fairness to all?

III. What types of written final exam might we have?

IV. What are the advantages and disadvantages of each?

V. What will be the form of our written final exam?

ENLIGHTENMENT DISCUSSIONS

The examples of organized and unorganized discussions at the beginning of this chapter came from enlightenment groups. Such groups have no need to reach agreement on values, courses of action, or belief. What is sought is a fuller understanding, a wider grasp of information pertinent to a topic, or consideration of a problem from as many points of view as possible. With no need for consensus or decision making, a wholly different pattern of group thinking is called for in most cases.[10]

General Principles for Patterning Learning Discussions

Keep the focus on common experience. Effective learning discussion grows out of a common body of experiences. All discussants should be reading the same articles or books, looking at the same painting or movie, observing the same group of children, or perhaps studying the same problem. Meaningful enlightenment discussions evolve from differing perceptions of such phenomena, supplemented by events or data experienced by one or a few group members. Each will see the same events somewhat differently, and each will differ in interpretations and evaluations.

The secret of productive learning discussion is to focus on what has been observed by all discussants. It has been found that members of study-discussion groups were more satisfied with the leadership and with the discussion and learned to qualify their judgments more often in groups which discussed topics most closely relevant to the assigned readings. Members of groups which discussed many topics peripheral to the readings did not show as much satisfaction or as much learning.[11]

Limit the number of issues or topics. Greater learning and more satisfaction were also found in groups where the average number of distinguishable topics per two-hour discussion was less than eleven than in groups where the average was more than fourteen topics per meeting.[12] Jumping rapidly from topic to topic should be avoided. In general, it is unwise to plan to discuss more than three or four basic issues per hour. The only exception would be when discussing something such as a poem or short story, a painting, or perhaps a sculpture. A longer poem, movie, or book should be discussed for a longer time.

Be guided by the nature of the subject. The pattern for a learning discussion is usually inherent in the subject of discussion and the group purpose in discussing it. Thus, if a group desires to understand and appreciate poetry, the pattern would emerge from that purpose and the poem. A group discussing a film might well discuss such char-

---

[10]The author has observed and studied many learning discussions, and has participated in workshops, seminars, training programs, bull sessions, and classroom discussions. He has planned training programs for literally hundreds of leaders of study-discussion groups. From these experiences and discussions with people in similar roles he has formulated some definite principles and procedures for organizing learning discussions.

[11]John K. Brilhart, "An Exploratory Study of Relationships between the Evaluating Process and Associated Behaviors of Participants in Six Study-Discussion Groups" (Ph.D. dissertation, Pennsylvania State University, 1962), pp. 283-293.

[12]*Ibid.*, pp. 275-282.

acteristics as the truthfulness of the theme, the acting, the staging, the photography, and their enjoyment of the film. A group seeking to understand differences in conceptions of God might discuss Catholic beliefs, various Protestant beliefs and Jewish beliefs. Or, they might compare each major religion by focusing on images of God, beliefs concerning divine purpose, and man's relation to God. A group seeking to understand the problems of open and fair housing for all citizens might use a problem-solving outline (even though the discussants would not necessarily seek a solution).

Specific Patterns

Specific patterns for organizing an enlightenment discussion are, for the most part, similar to those used to organize an informative public speech. We will consider them one at a time.

Topical or Major Issues

This is the most common pattern for learning discussions. The group discusses a set of topics or issues, each of which can be phrased as a question. These should be the basic issues which must be understood for members to achieve their purposes. While a designated leader should prepare a set of questions and subquestions to guide exploration of the major issues, he should never insist that the group discuss all of his questions or only his questions. The group must decide what issues will be discussed. One of the best techniques is to ask the group members to list the topics or issues they think should be discussed so that they can understand the topic. These issues can be written on a chart or board. As an alternative, the leader can suggest the issues and ask if the discussants want to omit any of them or add others.

Two examples will be presented to show this pattern of organization. The first is from a group that was discussing motion pictures. After seeing each film they used the following outline:

  I. What was the reaction to the theme of the picture?
 II. How good was the acting?
III. How well was the picture staged and costumed?
IV. How effective were lighting and photography?
 V. Would we recommend this picture to our friends?

After reading about the United States and communism, a group studying American foreign policy discussed the following issues during a two-hour meeting:

  I. How feasible is a policy of coexistence?
 II. How feasible is a policy of containment?
III. How feasible is a policy of liberation for communist-dominated countries?
 IV. What should be the main tenets of American foreign policy toward communist states?
  V. What are the differences in the policies of J. F. Dulles and C. Herter as Secretaries of State?
 VI. Which policy do we prefer?

These six questions were partly planned by the designated discussion leader, and part of them emerged from the group's interests and reactions to their readings.

Chronological

When discussing a historical trend, the subject can best be dealt with in a time sequence. Consider the following typical outline:

  I. How did the U. S. treat Indians while the country was being settled?
 II. How did it treat them during the heyday of the reservation system?
III. How are we treating them now?
 IV. What should be done for the Indians in the future?

A series of subquestions were discussed under each of these general issues. They dealt with such topics as treaties, legal contracts, citizenship, finances, discrimination, health and education.

Organization for a Fine Arts Discussion

Many learning groups, both in and out of the classroom, have found enlightenment and pleasure in discussing such works of art as poetry, paintings, short stories, pieces of sculpture or buildings. The staff of the Center for Continuing Liberal Education of the Pennsylvania State University worked out a basic sequence for such discussions. This format has proven to be helpful in countless discussions. Here is the basic format: (1) group examines the work of art together; (2) group discusses what they perceive in the work of art and what it means to them; (3) group again examines the work of art. Relatively little time will be spent discussing the artist, his motives or his life. If artistic techniques are considered, they are left until near the end of the discussion.

The following set of question may be used to guide the discussion of a poem. With modifications, the same questions could be used to discuss any other art form. With any specific work, some of the questions may be fruitless or meaningless, and others may be needed to open up avenues of perception and thought. Whatever questions are discussed, you should be careful to relate talk to the actual work of art (e.g., "What do certain words of the poem contribute to what I perceive?"). Most of the time should be spent on ideas relevant to the work of art which the group finds fruitful to discuss; no previous beliefs about how one ought to react to a poem or painting should block discussion of meaningful, relevant approaches to the work.

Introduction: A member of the group reads the poem aloud.

I. What situation occurs in the poem?
   A. What is actually taking place? What do you see in the poem?
   B. What other actions are described by the people in the poem?

II. How does the speaker in the poem feel about the situation he is discussing?
   A. At the beginning of the poem?
   B. In the middle?
   C. At the end?
   D. What is the nature and direction of the change of his feelings?

III. What kind of person does the speaker appear to be in the poem?
   A. What kind of person would feel as he feels?
   B. What kind of person would change as he does (or remain unchanged)?
   C. Is there any indication that poet and speaker differ in their ideas, personalities or feelings?

IV. What broad generalizations underlie the poem?
   A. What ideas does the poet assume to be true?
   B. Does he arrive at any insights, answers or solutions?
   C. How do we feel about these generalizations?

Conclusion: A group member reads the poem aloud.

Other Patterns for Learning Discussions

Other patterns of thought commonly used for organizing informative speeches can also guide learning-group discussions. A group discussing, "How serious is crime in our country today?" might use a *spatial* organization:

    I. How extensive and serious is crime in our city?

   II. How serious and extensive is it in our state?

 III. How serious and extensive is it in the country as a whole?

If the focus was on the causes of crime, a group would then use a *causal* organization, emphasizing causes and effects. For example:

  I. How extensive is crime in our cities?

 II. What factors have produced this amount of crime?
- A. Social organization and change?
- B. Law enforcement and legal procedures?
- C. Norms, beliefs and values?
- D. Other causes?

A *comparative* pattern might be used to compare two or more policies, objects, organizations and so forth. The group might begin by discussing criteria and goals, or with the first of the topics to be compared. For example, a group of students could discuss the merits of various teaching-learning approaches they have experienced while using the following outline:

   I. What are the advantages and disadvantages of lecturing?

  II. What are the advantages and disadvantages of discussions?

 III. What are the advantages and disadvantages of seminar or tutorial methods?

 IV. What are the advantages and disadvantages of programmed instruction?

A group wanting to learn as much as possible about a particular problem could use the problem-solving pattern without trying to come to a decision. All major proposed solutions would be discussed, but no attempt would be made to reach a final solution.

Regardless of the pattern used to organize thinking and talking in a learning discussion, it should reflect the basic purpose, which is learning, reflect the basic issues of the topic or question being discussed, reflect the particular interests and needs of the group members. To get a better understanding of these principles and how they are applied in a given situation, you may want to prepare a set of leader's outlines on problems and topics to which each type of organization is appropriate, then engage in such discussions with your friends or classmates. Each discussion and outline should be followed by observer and group evaluation.

BIBLIOGRAPHY

Barnlund, Dean C., and Haiman, Franklyn S., *The Dynamics of Discussion*, Boston: Houghton Mifflin Company, 1960.

Dewey, John, *How We Think*, Boston: D. C. Heath and Company, 1933.

Lee, Irving J., *How to Talk with People*, New York: Harper and Brothers, 1952.

Maier, Norman R. F., *Problem-solving Discussions and Conferences*, New York: McGraw-Hill Book Company, 1963.

Osborn, Alex F., *Applied Imagination* (rev. ed.), New York: Charles Scribner's Sons, 1957.

Parnes, Sidney F., and Harding, Harold F. (eds.), *A Source Book for Creative Thinking*, New York: Charles Scribner's Sons, 1962.

Utterback, William E., *Group Thinking and Conference Leadership* (rev. ed.), New York: Holt, Rinehart and Winston, Inc., 1964.

EXERCISES

1. Write three problem questions which might be discussed by a small group from your class. Present these either to your instructor or to a group of classmates for evaluation in the following areas: clarity, problem or solution, area of freedom of the class, competence of class.

2. Select one of the above questions or one which is assigned by your instructor. Write three different leader's outlines for guiding discussion on this problem: one using the creative problem-solving sequence, one using the basic reflective-thinking sequence and one using a more detailed reflective-thinking pattern. Compare your outlines with those done by three or four classmates, then construct one outline acceptable to all of you.

3. With an observer to report how orderly the discussion appears to be, actually discuss the problem, following the outline agreed upon by your group.

4. Select a subject of interest to the entire class, then write a leader's outline for a learning discussion on this subject. Subject it to scrutiny by instructor and classmates.

5. Plan a strategy for leading discussion of a short poem of your own selection. If there is time, have three or four poems discussed by subgroups of classmates. In each discussion evaluate orderliness, enjoyment and learning.

Chapter 4

PREPARING TO DISCUSS

"A discussion is a group of people, none of whom is individually capable of doing anything, deciding collectively that nothing can be done." The wag who coined this definition must have listened to many of the verbal interchanges which pass for problem-solving discussion. Perhaps it is because we discuss at the drop of a hat in daily contacts that so many people look upon discussion as something which no one (except possibly a leader) would prepare for.

But effective discussion, like effective public speaking, grows out of dependable knowledge and clear thinking, which can come only from preparation. Of course there are productive discussions for which nobody seems to have made specific preparations. But appearances here, as in many situations, are deceiving. Participating in such discussions are people who by nature of their work, life and study are well prepared: a group of speech teachers discussing how to help students overcome initial stage fright, political science majors talking about reforms needed in the city charter, or a group of dog fanciers talking about how to keep a dog comfortable in hot weather. These people are informed and have done much thinking in advance of their discussion. But even the experts can do a better job if they prepare specifically. For example, what self-respecting engineer would fail to prepare for a discussion to plan changes in automobile brakes?

Effective group discussion is never a pool of ignorance. Success is contingent on the degree to which the group is informed. Every dependable conclusion, solution, interpretation or belief rests on dependable evidence and valid reasoning from the evidence. Half-informed participants can reach only half-baked decisions. The valuable participant has plumbed his subject deeply. Think for a moment of a group of college students trying to discuss intelligently such topics as capital punishment or the control of atomic arms without having studied the topic. Would you place credence in the findings of such a group?

Groups are frequently plagued by playboys who keep telling irrelevant jokes or pulling the group off the topic. Such nuisances are almost always poorly informed. One promoter of study-discussion programs advocated the policy that, "If anyone has not read the materials, he is not permitted to speak unless to ask a question." Needless to say, this policy produced prepared participants and satisfying discussions. Many study-discussion leaders report that when the participants have not prepared, the ensuing discussion is listless, disorganized, shallow and frustrating.

The contrast between being uninformed and informed was discovered by a group of students at a large university. They began attacking the university food service, with a host of complaints about what was wrong and what should be done to improve it. Fortunately, they soon realized that they knew very little about the facts of the subject except for what they had seen and heard as students and customers. Thus, they decided to conduct a careful investigation. The labor was divided among the group members, some studying menu planning, others studying food preparation, others looking into costs, and others investigating food service at other schools. Information was gathered from home economists, dieticians, food service employees, journals and books. At the next meeting this group of informed students pooled their knowledge, and came to the conclusion that they had the finest food service of any university in their section of the country, that meals were reasonably priced, that menus were better planned than most family diets, and that many of the complaints were due to ignorance or to misuse of the food service by students. The problem soon changed to, "How can we get the students at our university to appreciate the excellence of our food service, and to take better advantage of it?" They also made a few recommendations for minor improvements in the food service, all based on facts of the case. These suggestions were well received by the man in charge of the service, who expressed his appreciation and put several of them into effect.

Since preparation is so important, the question now becomes, "What can we do to prepare ourselves to discuss effectively?" No answer will suffice for all occasions, but a plan for preparing to engage in group problem solving, a plan for preparing to engage in group learning discussion, and suggestions for preparing one's self to engage in other types of discussions will be presented next. The last section of this chapter is devoted to the special preparations which should be made by a designated leader, including notices, preparation of facilities, and group planning sessions.

PREPARING FOR PROBLEM-SOLVING DISCUSSIONS

Each member of a problem-solving or decision-making group should prepare himself for effective discussion. The steps suggested below are arranged in the order in which they should be taken. This procedure may be modified somewhat as you become more experienced in discussion or if you are unusually expert in the problem area. But *none of these steps can be omitted* without a loss in effectiveness. Also, the *order* in which preparation takes place is vital.

1. *Review and organize your own stock of information and ideas on the subject.* Undoubtedly you already have some information and experience on the subject, or you would not be discussing it. Taking a systematic inventory of this knowledge can save you much time in preparation, and will enable you to recall what you need when you need to. To begin reading at this point would be wasteful and inefficient.

a.   Place the problem or subject in perspective. To what is it related? What will it affect, or by what is it affected? For example, in trying to plan a scholarship program for a corporation, one should consider the corporation's financial condition, long-range plans, obligations to the community, public relations, types of employees and the like.

b.   Make an inventory of what you know about the subject. An approach that may help you recall is to list courses taken, jobs held, reports, firsthand experiences, articles read, books, ideas and so forth. Additional headings will suggest themselves as you proceed. These headings can be put on sheets of scratch paper. Then jot down in brief form everything that comes to mind. Let your mind be "freewheeling," without being concerned with degree of importance, relevance, or even validity.

c.   Organize your information into a problem-solving outline. This can be in a rough pencil draft. Look over your notes for main issues, topics or questions about the problem, being guided by a model outline suggested in Chapter 3.

d.   Look for deficiencies. Your outline of information will reveal just what you do *not* know, where specific information is needed, and which ideas or opinions are unsupported.

2. *Gather needed information.* You are now ready to plan research to correct some of the deficiencies in your knowledge and thinking. We will review briefly the means for getting this information and recording it, for this topic has probably been covered previously in your speech and English classes.

Information and ideas slip from memory or twist themselves in recall unless we make *accurate* and *complete notes.* Carrying books, magazines and recordings to a discussion would at best be clumsy, and you might get so lost in the mess that you distract your group.

The best system of note taking is to record each bit of information or idea on a separate 3 by 5 note card. Put a topic heading on the card, followed by the specific subject. Then list exact details of the source, just as you would for a bibliography. Finally, record the information, idea or quotation. The following example shows how to do this:

PREPARING TO DISCUSS   Get General Understanding First

    Harnack, R. Victor and Fest, Thorrel B., Group Discussion: Theory and Technique New York: Appleton-Century-Crofts, 1964, pp. 118-119.
    "Unless the member is already rather thoroughly acquainted with the nature of the problem to be solved, he ought to spend some time investigating the nature of the overall problem before he begins looking for the specific evidence that is his assignment. . . . Looking at the whole problem will help the individual in three ways. First, he will be better able to fit his specific assignment into the total picture. Second, he will be prepared to understand and evaluate the contributions made by others with different assignments. Third, he may discover some evidence or ideas that may have escaped the notice of those investigating the other aspects of the problem."

The note cards provide both accuracy and flexibility. One can arrange them in various groups as he synthesizes and interprets the evidence he has collected. They can be consulted with ease during discussion without having to leaf through a disorganized notebook. Full reference data permit others to evaluate the credibility of the evidence. It is virtually useless to say something appeared in *The New York Times* or *Newsweek* or a book by some psychologist.

Your information may come from many sources:

    a. *Personal observation* When feasible, gather information firsthand. For example, before discussing how to reduce traffic jams on a campus, you will want to look at the traffic flow from the perspective of your problem and the questions you have generated.

    b. *Interviews* Where you can see only a small part or where you are not sufficiently knowledgeable to observe meaningfully, inquire of people who are trained observers or who have firsthand contact with your problem. For example, you could ask the police about the nature and extent of the jams, and you could ask students and faculty how they feel about the problem.

    c. *Reading* On many topics, the biggest pool of information will be found in books, journals, newspapers and other printed pages. You will need to read widely and thoroughly. The *Reader's Guide to Periodical Literature*, the *New York Times Index,* and the card catalog of your library can help you compile a bibliography. Often much labor can be saved in a group by dividing up a bibliography, so that a few key materials are read by all discussants but most writings are examined by one or two members.

Read wisely. Instead of reading an entire book, look in the index and table of contents for clues to what is pertinent. Skim rapidly until you find something of value to your group's special purpose. Read the summary of an article to see if the entire article warrants your time.

d. *Other sources* One of the best ways to get ideas and information is to talk to your acquaintances about the problem you are investigating. Listen for new ideas, expression of feeling and specific information which you can later check for validity. Useful information and ideas may crop up anywhere or anytime, perhaps when least expected. You may find something in a television program, from a lecture, or from a radio show. Keep your ears open and a supply of note cards handy.

3. *Evaluate your information and ideas.* In the light of all you have learned in individual research of the problem, it is now time to evaluate your information and ideas. Many of your ideas may have collapsed before new evidence. Some of your information may be spurious, in direct conflict with other information, or from highly suspect sources. Some will be virtually irrelevant to the problem facing the group. Now is the time to cull the misleading, false, suspect, unsubstantiated or irrelevant so you do not misinform, confuse or delay your group.

A careful review of all you have collected will help you get rid of useless material. Apply tests of evidence to all the data you have collected, and thus eliminate the suspect and downright false.[1] You will always want to ask the following:

Are these data reasonable?

Is the source relatively free from bias?

Was the source in a position to observe, and capable of accurate observations?

Are these data in agreement with those from other sources?

If an opinion, is the source a recognized expert in the field?

In the case of statistics is the method of collecting data made clear? Is the method of computing averages explained? Was the sampling procedure employed likely to give an accurate picture?[2]

4. *Reorganize your information and ideas.* Form a tentative discussion outline, using the major headings for a problem-solving pattern.

---

[1]For an explanation of such tests, see Austin J. Freeley, *Argumentation and Debate* (San Francisco: Wadsworth Publishing Company, Inc., 1961), Chapter 6.

[2]For a simple explanation of dangers in statistical data, see Darrell C. Huff, *How to Lie with Statistics* (New York: W. W. Norton & Company, Inc., 1954).

Arrange your cards into piles (clarifying and limiting the problem, describing and analyzing the problem, criteria, possible solutions and evaluating the solutions). Then the material helping you to clarify and analyze the problem can be further arranged according to details or symptoms of the problem, contributing factors and the like. This arrangement will simplify the writing of your outline.

Your outline may contain some possible solutions; doubtless it should. You may have some evidence and reasoning which shows how similar solutions were tried on similar problems. You may even have some suggestions on how to put a plan into effect, how to check to see if it works, and perhaps how to make adjustments. However, such thinking and planning is tentative. The worst sort of preparation is to go to a group discussion prepared to advocate a particular solution against all comers. Just as bad is to feel that one's personal definition and understanding of the problem is the complete problem. If researching and outlining make a participant close minded, it is better he remains ignorant. At least he will not deadlock the group, and perhaps he can listen and learn from others. Remember that the experts in almost any field, the people at the very frontier of knowledge, are the least dogmatic and sure of themselves. From these people the discussant who has read widely, thought long, and made his detailed outline should take heed. At the best he will now be prepared to contribute some reliable information, some ideas for testing in the forge of the group's collective knowledge and thinking, and perhaps most important, to listen with more understanding, to ask knowing questions, and thus to shape an image of and a solution to the problem. No one person could devise all of this alone.

PREPARING FOR ENLIGHTENMENT DISCUSSION

Much of what has been said about preparing for a problem-solving discussion applies also to preparing one's self for participation in a learning discussion. Certainly one needs to take stock of his experience and knowledge, to organize and to investigate the subject more fully. Outlining information may be omitted in some cases, or if done, the form of the outline would now be according to one of the patterns suggested for organizing group learning discussions.

Preparation for enlightenment discussion will vary depending on the nature of the subject and the group purposes. Usually there is a program of necessary reading. All members of the group discussing a subject need some common background. One should first attempt to get an overview of the subject, perhaps by reading a general article or by skimming an entire set of readings, an entire chapter, book or whatever is to be discussed. Then the discussant should either be guided by a study outline prepared for the group, or else should himself prepare questions to answer as he reads. For example, before reading an article by the late Secretary of State, John Foster Dulles, one might ask such questions as, "What does Dulles think should be our relationship with Latin America?," "What evidence does he give to support his belief?," "What does he predict will happen if we do not follow his policy?"[3]

When preparing to discuss a controversial topic your reading should encompass as many contrasting interpretations or points of view as possible. To *learn*, we must consider that which *does not conform* with our present beliefs; we must perceive, accept and adapt to new knowledge. *This is most difficult to do.* We tend to listen to people who believe as we do, and to read what we want to read. We tend to be undercritical of these sources, and to be overcritical of evidence or opinions contrary to what we know and believe. It has been proven that we forget new evidence or beliefs that are different from our own.[4] While reading, the study-discussant should make notes of the following:

> The significant issues he feels should be discussed.
>
> The controversial points of view that are to be examined by all discussants.
>
> The passages which are unclear to him.
>
> Any questions he wants to raise.
>
> How this reading compares with other readings on the subject.
>
> How this relates to his life and how it compares with his experience and reasoning.
>
> Any other relevant information or experience that comes to mind.

Thus armed, he will now be a most valuable member of the discussion group. He will be able to understand the comments and questions raised by others. He will be prepared to help guide the discussion into the most important issues. He will see that the questions which concern him are discussed. And he will recognize the limitations of his own points of view and those of others.

When the discussion is designed to explore works of art, study the art carefully, shifting the focus as you do. With a painting, you might

---

[3]If you think this procedure is like the famous SQ3R method of studying, you are right!

[4]Sir Frederic Bartlett, *Thinking: An Experimental and Social Study* (New York: Basic Books, Inc., Publishers, 1958).

shift attention from outline, to color, to spaces, to planes, to texture and so forth. With a poem, you would first try to interpret it, then note how it is constructed, and finally form some tentative opinion of its worth or meaningfulness. Make notes of your questions and the stanzas which puzzle you; record your reactions. By all means, *read the poem aloud.*

In summary, focus on the materials — readings, visuals or whatever — which will be discussed. Look at the subject of your forthcoming discussion from as many angles and points of view as possible, deferring final judgment. And most important, put yourself into the preparation — what do you see, understand, feel or believe in response? Put down the most important of your observations and musings in brief notes as a possible springboard for remarks during the discussion. Then go to the group meeting in a mood of inquiry, ready to discover, not to persuade.

THE LEADER'S SPECIAL PREPARATIONS

Regardless of the type of discussion, when there is time for advance planning and preparation, a designated discussion leader (be he called chairman, moderator, etc.) has a special responsibility to help the participants by coordinating group preparation. This may include planning an agenda, seeing that each discussant is notified or reminded of the meeting, planning the pattern for guiding the discussion of each problem, making resource materials available, and making clear what is expected of each participant.

When possible, each participant should receive a notice of the meeting far enough in advance so he can prepare himself sufficiently. The nature and timing of this notice will depend on the details of the discussion and the basis for the group's existence. A chairman of a newly appointed committee might call the members to find a suitable time for them to meet, then send a notice to each member somewhat like the following:

This notice gives the members the exact time and place of the meeting, expected participants, purpose of the meeting, preparation, and some basic information about the task.

Sometimes a designated leader will need to plan an agenda of problems to be dealt with by a group. He might ask the discussants what problems the group should deal with, then arrange an agenda which will be sent to all members in time for them to prepare. For example, when the author was scheduled to participate in a panel which was to explore ways to train adult leaders, he was invited by the chairman to submit questions for the discussion. The chairman synthesized all

---

July 23, 1966

From: Charles Porter, Chairman of the Library Committee

To: Walter Brown, Helen Davis, Michael Rubenstein and Betty Yalnoske

Subject: Meeting of Committee to Explore Loss of Library Materials

     We will meet in room 24-B of the University Library at 9:30 a.m. on Friday, July 29.

     The purpose of the meeting is twofold: to plan our work and to make an initial assessment of the nature and extent of the problem facing us.

     The attached sheet summarizes what the Librarian has been able to tell me about the problem. Try to gather as much information as you can about the nature, extent, and causes of the loss and mutilation of library holdings. Please be prepared to discuss what you think we need to know and any ideas you may have about how we can get this information.

---

the suggested questions into a five-question outline. This outline, along with the time and place of the public meeting and some suggestions for preparation, was sent to all panelists. The result was that the panelists were well prepared for and satisfied with the discussion.

Sometimes a designated leader may find it feasible to call a preliminary meeting of the group in order to plan an agenda or perhaps to plan how the group will get the information it needs. At such a meeting the group would clarify the problem facing them, decide what information they need and how to get it, and divide up the work of research. It is always important to convene a panel or other public discussion group before they face the audience. Even if it is just before the discussion is presented, the members can be introduced to each other, the pattern of questions to be discussed can be made clear to all, and procedures can be explained. Such a meeting should not include a rehearsal; this will make you sound stale to the audience.

The designated leader of a study-discussion group has the special responsibility of working out a plan or pattern for guiding the discussion he will later suggest to the group. He will need both a set of questions about the basic issues and follow-up questions to help bring out details; he will need excerpts of readings, points of view, and feelings. For example, in a film discussion part of the leader's preparation outline might look like this:

I. What did we think of the acting?
  A. How effective was Montgomery Clift?
    1. Did the character seem consistent?
    2. Do you agree with his interpretation? Why or why not?
    3. What feelings or insights did he arouse in you?
  B. How did you feel about the acting of Burt Lancaster?
    1. Was his role believable?
    2. Was he consistent?
    3. What techniques or approaches were especially important?
    4. How did you feel about his acting?

Sometimes the leader of a learning-discussion group is given a manual or outline (supplied by a film distributor, course, film strip or TV series). In using it, the leader is wise to study the materials for the discussion first, making notes about what he considers to be the major questions and issues. Only then should he turn to the leader's guide, comparing the suggested questions with his own. As a general rule, it is best to use your own questions even though these may be primarily adaptations of questions suggested in the manual. Finally, arrange the questions you select into outline form.

PHYSICAL ARRANGEMENTS

An otherwise effective discussion can almost be ruined by poor physical arrangements. Someone, usually the designated leader, must see that facilities have been prepared.

Private Discussions

The optimum for private discussion is a circular seating arrangement with members seated close together. In most discussions, each member should also have a writing surface. If the group meets in a classroom with flexible seating, have the participants push chairs into a circle (or a semicircle where everyone can see the chalkboard). In a room with fixed seating, a few portable chairs can be brought in or some participants can sit sideways in their chairs. If you have a long rectangular table, get the people at the middle of each side to push their chairs out from the table, giving an oval seating pattern. At a square table, try to avoid seating anyone at the corners. Four to six small tables can be pulled into an arrangement approximating a circle.

If group members are not well acquainted, each should be given a name "tent" on which to write or print his name on both sides. A plain 5 by 8 file card makes a good name "tent" when folded lengthwise. It is then set in front of the discussant so all members of the group can readily see it and address him by name. Be sure the writing is large and dark.

Whenever smoking is permitted, each discussant should have easy access to an ash tray. Unless someone is seriously annoyed by smoke or smoking is prohibited, it should be permitted.

In many discussions it will be advisable to place a small note pad and pencil at each seat. Of course, in a classroom each student is expected to come equipped to take notes.

Whenever possible, problem-solving groups (and many learning groups) should have either a chalkboard or an easel with large newsprint-chart pads. This should be located where everyone can see it and where it is convenient for the designated leader or recorder to use it. Be sure that a supply of chalk or crayons is on hand. Chart pads have the advantage of permitting the group recorder to keep notes visible to all; later he can use these to write up a report on the group's findings, ideas and decisions.

If any special visual materials are to be used, be sure they are prepared and in good working order: enough handouts to go around, charts arranged in the order in which they will be displayed, film projector threaded and focused, slides in correct order, or record player warmed up.

Adequate lighting, comfortable temperature, and ventilation should be arranged as it would be for any meeting. The room should be quiet and free from intruders. The writer has seen several meetings thrown off track by someone wandering into a library room, children playing in an adjoining room, or workmen passing through. Extravagance is not important, but comfort, convenience and freedom from distraction are essential.

Public Discussions

Public discussions call for special arrangements. When staging a live-audience public discussion, it is important that all discussants be in view of each other and of the audience at all times. Only with this arrangement can a sense of direct interaction occur. To accomplish this, seat the discussants in a semicircle, usually with the moderator at the center. The audience then faces the panel, and the panelists can alternately face the audience and each other. Panelists should be seated behind a table, preferably with some sort of cover on the front of it. Two small tables in an open "V" make an excellent arrangement.

A large name card should be placed on the table in front of each panelist. If the room is large and microphones are needed, they should be in sufficient number and so placed that the panelists can largely ignore them. Neck microphones can be used. If a chalkboard or easel is available, it is a good idea to display the topic or question being discussed; sometimes the major issues or questions can also be listed. Such visual devices help auditors keep the discussion organized and clear in their minds.

In a very large assembly it may be necessary to have floor microphones for a forum discussion. If so, these should be strategically placed and their use clearly explained to the audience before the forum begins. If not essential, do not use them. They will inhibit some people, and can lead to much confusion and delay.

The theme of this chapter has been that effective discussion comes from people who have prepared themselves to discuss. By getting as broad a perspective as possible on the group topic, discussants are at once informed, yet humble in the knowledge that they are only partially informed. It has been pointed out that good group thinking can only come from good individual thinking. Leaders have a special responsibility to help discussants prepare. Finally, a group must have physical arrangements which will facilitate a productive interchange. No book can tell you exactly how to prepare for a specific discussion, but you can take certain steps which, modified to suit the situation, can greatly increase the probability of a successful and satisfying discussion.

Bibliography

Freeley, Austin J., *Argumentation and Debate*, Belmont, Calif.: Wadsworth Publishing Company, Inc., 1961, Ch. VI.

Harnack, R. Victor, and Fest, Thorrel B., *Group Discussion: Theory and Technique*, New York: Appleton-Century-Crofts, 1964, Ch. V & VI.

Huff, Darrell C., *How to Lie with Statistics*, New York: W. W. Norton & Company, Inc., 1954.

Zelko, Harold P., *Successful Conference and Discussion Techniques*, New York: McGraw-Hill Book Company, 1957.

EXERCISES

1. Write a notice for a committee meeting, one for a learning discussion, and one for a panel discussion.
2. Plan how to arrange your meeting room for a problem-solving discussion by the entire class and for three or four simultaneous

problem-solving discussions by subgroups of the class. Put your plans in the form of diagrams.

3. Plan and diagram the physical arrangements for a panel discussion in each of three settings: your classroom, an auditorium and a large lounge with informal seating.

4. In class select a topic of interest to all.
   a. Prepare a bibliography of resource materials on the topic.
   b. Prepare yourself to discuss the subject, including a detailed outline and note cards to be submitted to your instructor following the discussion.

5. Select three short poems to discuss with six other members of your class. Prepare a general leader's outline for guiding the discussion of each poem. Select one of these poems for actual discussion, and supply each member of your group with a copy at least two days before the discussion.

Chapter 5

EFFECTIVE DISCUSSION LEADERSHIP

The idea that leadership is important to any group is generally accepted. The style and method of leadership have been matters of increasing concern to small-group researchers and theorists since the early 1940s. Prior to that time it was widely believed that leaders were specially gifted people who were "born to lead," and that there was little anyone could do to develop leadership skills. Despite research findings to the contrary, we often act as if we believed there were some mystical quality of leadership which, if possessed, makes one a leader in virtually any situation. Generals are assumed to be capable of supplying effective leadership in education or government; football captains are elected to class offices; great teachers are made chairmen of committees — and all too often the results are dismal.

People who keep abreast of research in leadership — and there has been a vast amount of it in recent years — know better. Leadership is not a quality or personality trait; leadership skills can be learned. Training people to diagnose and supply the changing leadership functions needed by a group has made many organizations more productive. Businesses constantly look for people able to work with and lead others, then give them further specialized training in human relations, sensitivity, conference leadership, group dynamics, and leadership. The armed forces conduct extensive training and retraining programs in leadership skills for officers of all ranks. Community action groups develop grassroots leadership through elaborate training programs. Unions conduct leadership-training programs, often in conjunction with universities, to develop skills in their rank-and-file. In short, there is a great demand for people skilled at leading, and to develop such people a lot of money is spent on training.

Money and time spent on developing discussion-leadership skills are invested wisely. As we have seen, discussion is fundamental to democratic organization and cooperation. No discussion group can be effective without appropriate leadership — and that means skilled leaders. Whenever a group has a designated leader (either elected or appointed), he can almost literally "make or break" the group.

What is expected of the designated discussion leader? What should be his relationship to the rest of the group members if he is to maximize satisfaction and productivity? In this chapter, we will first consider the concepts leader and leadership; second, principles of effective leadership in discussion; third, a philosophy of leadership and leadership style; fourth, the special responsibilities and techniques of a discussion leader.

LEADERS AND LEADERSHIP

It is quite possible for a discussion group to have no single leader and yet to have excellent leadership. It is also possible for a discussion group to have a leader and yet be woefully lacking in leadership. If these statements seem paradoxical, it is only because the terms *leader* and *leadership* are confusing due to overlapping meanings.

Leadership refers to any behavior which helps a group clarify and achieve group goals. Social scientists are virtually unanimous in defining leadership as *influence*. The definition given by Tannenbaum, Weschler, and Massarik is typical: "We define leadership as *interpersonal influence, exercised in situation and directed, through the communication process, toward the attainment of a specified goal or goals.*"[1] Only that influence which is directed toward group goals will be called group leadership, thereby excluding behavior in which one member influences another to work apart from or contrary to the good of the group. Excluded would be influence irrelevant to group goals, such as one member emulating the mannerisms of another or getting another to join him for refreshments after a meeting (unless that act is to achieve greater harmony in the group). Likewise, the use of force, threat or power to influence another to comply will not be called group leadership. Leadership is not exercised when a follower has no choice but to obey or be harmed; that is compulsion.

Discussion leadership is the responsibility of all members; it will usually be shared by several of them. It is now believed the tasks which were considered to be the sole responsibility of the leader (introducing

---

[1]Robert Tannenbaum, Irving R. Weschler, and Fred Massarik, *Leadership and Organizations A Behavioral Science Approach* (New York: McGraw-Hill Book Company, 1961), p. 24.

the problem, guiding the discussion, probing, spreading participation, clarifying, resolving disagreements, asking questions, etc.) can better be handled by many members of a group. Some people may have more skills at certain leadership tasks, have special knowledge, or have more sensitivity to what the designated leader has missed. If so a leadership team emerges.

The term *leader* may be used to refer to any person who exerts influence in the group, any person who exerts more than average influence or any person who is designated (by appointment or election) to exert leadership and who consequently becomes a focal point for interaction and group procedures. Most discussion groups are more efficient and democratic if there is a designated leader. But such a designated leader is wise to encourage others to be leaders (in the sense of exerting more than average influence) according to their skills and the needs of the group. To emphasize this point, Bales found that task and social leadership can rarely be performed equally well by the same person.[2] In a particular group, then, there may be several persons who are leaders: one who gets the group oriented, some who supply needed information, others who take the lead in finding ideas, and others who harmonize conflict and reduce tensions.

The preceding paragraph does not imply that a discussion group does not need a designated leader. A designated leader has a special responsibility to maintain perspective and to see that all needed leadership services are performed. However, the ideal is a group in which most leadership functions are shared, with the designated leader doing whatever is necessary since no one else can do it well. The proportion of the total leadership which he supplies will vary greatly, depending on the way in which the group was formed, the expectations of the members, the nature of the task, the skills of the leader and other members, and other variables. In a one-meeting group the designated leader will likely do most of the organizing, clarifying, summarizing and other procedural tasks; concomitantly, he will probably do little suggesting or evaluating of ideas. In a continuing group, routines will develop with members taking on specialized roles; after a time, the designated leader may be able to participate very much like any other member. As members take on tasks of leadership and develop skill in them, the designated leader's proportion of leadership will decline.

---

[2]Robert F. Bales, "Task Roles and Social Roles in Problem Solving Groups," in E. E. Maccoby, T. M. Newcomb, and E. L. Hartley (eds.), *Reading in Social Psychology*, 3rd ed. (New York: Henry Holt and Company, 1958), pp. 437-447.

SOME CHARACTERISTICS OF EFFECTIVE DISCUSSION LEADERS

What are the characteristics of an effective designated leader of discussion groups? The answer depends on many factors, and not at all on some mystical quality called leadership ability. From research it is possible to summarize many forces which determine the leadership of an effective discussion group without getting involved in general theories of leadership. By developing the characteristics discussed in the following paragraphs, there is much you can do to enhance your chances of success as a discussion leader.

Effective discussion leaders are skilled in organizing group thinking. Wilson found that persons who emerged as effective problem-solving discussion leaders had a much better than average grasp of the process of reflective thinking.[3] Brilhart found that study-discussion leaders selected by participants as future leaders were unusually skilled in organizing discussions.[4] To be an effective leader of discussions, you will need to become familiar with patterns for group thinking, be able to suggest an appropriate pattern to a group, be skilled at detecting tangents during discussion, and be able to bring the group back on track.

Effective discussion leaders are open-minded. The author found that study-discussion leaders chosen by participants as future leaders were much more conditional in the way they expressed judgments than were leaders not chosen as future leaders. Maier demonstrated that a leader who suspends judgment and encourages full consideration of minority points of view is more effective than one who does not.[5] The writer repeatedly gave "dogmatism" and "authoritarianism" tests to students in discussion classes, and found that students most often chosen as leaders by classmates tended to score much better on these measures of open-mindedness. Haiman reported similar findings for his classes when using these scales and an "open-mindedness" scale which he devised.[6] The picture is clear: Effective discussion leaders are more open-minded than average participants and can encourage open-minded consideration by participants.

Effective discussion leaders have a good grasp of the problem facing the group. Studies of leadership have repeatedly shown that persons

---

[3]Carl L. Wilson, "An Experimental Study of Selected Correlates of Emergent Leadership During Problem-Solving Discussion" (D. Ed. dissertation, Pennsylvania State College, 1953).

[4]John K. Brilhart, "An Exploratory Study of Relationships between the Evaluating Process and Associated Behavior of Participants in Six Study-Discussion Groups" (Ph.D. dissertation, Pennsylvania State University, 1962).

[5]Norman R. F. Maier, and A. R. Solem, "The Contributions of a Discussion Leader to the Quality of Group Thinking: The Effective Use of Minority Opinions," *Human Relations* 5 (1952), pp. 277-288.

[6]Franklyn S. Haiman, from a paper given at the Annual Convention of the Speech Association of America, December, 1964.

who emerge as leaders are exceptionally knowledgeable in the group task area. At the least, the leader must have a sufficient grasp of the subject to organize it and ask stimulating questions about it.

Effective discussion leaders have respect for and sensitivity to others. The discussion leader must trust the group and believe in its collective wisdom. He will act with tact and concern for the participants' feelings. He reacts to statements with acceptance; even when he may disagree personally, he will seek to know how they think and why. He will be careful not to attack the person when disagreeing; in the language of argumentation, he speaks *ad rem* (to the issue) rather than *ad hominem* (to the man, i.e., attacking his wisdom, integrity, or character). An effective leader is especially aware of how members feel during the discussion, noting when members are unhappy with the turn of events, when they are on the verge of a consensus, or when a hesitant member wants to speak. He will treat everyone with equal dignity, and never take sides in any personal conflict.

Effective discussion leaders are good listeners. The effective leader is actively involved in trying to understand and clarify what is not clear. He is patient and calm, not interrupting others (except maybe a dominating member). He can summarize accurately what has been said. He speaks in response to what other members say.

Effective discussion leaders speak well. Ability to speak clearly has been shown to be important to success in all social contexts. The able discussion leader speaks to the group as a whole in clear, impartial terms. His remarks are concise, organized and pertinent.

Effective discussion leaders are flexible. One who must proceed in a predetermined way, one who must follow his outline, cannot be an effective leader of discussion groups. Who can know what leadership skills other group members may have, or what they may feel? The leader must be sensitive to what is happening, then adjust his behavior and plans to do whatever is needed to help the group proceed steadily and efficiently toward the group goal.

Effective discussion leaders are calm and self-controlled. If the designated leader loses his temper, the group will invariably flounder without direction. Consider as a model the calm, accepting manner of the skilled judge who must maintain his perspective and control at all times.

Effective discussion leaders can take on distinctive roles. Many studies have shown that effective discussion leaders can take on roles distinctively different from those of other group members.[7] The author found the most effective study-discussion leaders were those who asked

---

[7]A. Paul Hare, *Handbook of Small Group Research* (New York: The Free Press of Glencoe, 1962), Chapter XI.

more questions, gave more procedural guidance and expressed fewer personal opinions than other members. Berkowitz found when task pressures were not urgent, conferees preferred a chairman whose role was distinct, characterized by strong procedural control.[8]

We could list many more characteristics of effective discussion leaders, such as ability to give credit to the group. But those listed seem to be the most important. Notice that all these characteristics *can be learned*. No man can be a paradigm of all virtues, but anyone who leads discussion groups can seek to develop himself in the directions indicated by the preceding list.

PHILOSOPHIES AND STYLES OF LEADERSHIP

How one acts as a discussion leader depends in large part on his philosophy of leadership. A large number of writers have described the differences between the styles of autocratic, democratic and laissez-faire leaders. These styles rest on distinct philosophies of leadership. Each will be described briefly, along with some other styles of leadership which are appropriate under special circumstances.

An autocratic discussion leader seeks to impose his will, belief or solution on the group. The result is a pseudodiscussion during which the group goes through the motions of discussion but the end result is predetermined by the leader. Under an autocrat, no one speaks unless permitted by the leader. Everyone's ideas are judged by the leader. He decides on the exact order of events on the agenda and the sequence in which a problem will be discussed. He may listen to advice but when he has made up his mind, the "group decision" has been made. Power resides in this one person rather than in the group. Such a leader rarely announces the agenda of a meeting in advance, nor does he often help inform members. Armed with a private agenda and as the only fully prepared person, he can readily dominate the other discussants. For example, an autocrat in the classroom decides just what aspects of a poem will be discussed, and the "right" interpretation of the poem.

The autocratically inclined leader, lacking the power of an absolute autocrat, may use all sorts of manipulative techniques to seduce agreement. He is interested in whatever will advance his ideas and purposes; he will interrupt and ignore or argue with anything to the contrary, often without trying to understand the other speaker's point of view. The autocrat distorts summaries toward his purpose and states ideas

---

[8]Leonard Berkowitz, "Sharing Leadership In Small, Decision-Making Groups," *Journal of Abnormal and Social Psychology* 48 (1953), pp. 231-238.

with highly emotive language. Sometimes he coerces an agreement by preventing the group from making a decision until time is almost gone, then pressures others to accept his solution. He will cut others out by talking loudly and rapidly, by interrupting and ridiculing. He may coerce participation by saying, "Joe, what do you think of that?" or "Joe, don't you agree?" Joe must answer or lose face.

On what assumptions would you base your personal style of leadership? An autocratic style rests on the beliefs that a few select men (of which the autocrat is one) are specially endowed, that the majority of men are incapable or irresponsible, that the way to get people to act is to give them personal rewards and punishments. Such premises underlie the governing techniques of Plato, Machiavelli, Nietzsche, Hitler, and discussion leaders who predetermine the results which their groups should reach.

The democratic discussion leader, in contrast to the autocratic leader, seeks to discover the group's will and facilitate its achievement. A discussion of this sort can never be predetermined by anyone, but will be the result of interaction. In democratic leadership, discussants speak when they want to. All ideas are treated as group property, and judgment of them is the responsibility of the entire group. All authority for decision making resides in the group. Influence comes primarily from information, ideas and skills in doing what is needed to achieve mutually acceptable goals. When discussion leadership is democratic, everyone has equal opportunity to prepare himself for discussion. Even establishing the agenda and the pattern for discussing a topic or problem is the prerogative of the group, not of a single member (or leader). All power exercised by the designated leader is granted him by the group for the group's good. Such a leader may suggest and encourage, but he never can compel, coerce or manipulate. Ideally, a designated leader's approval is no more important than that of any other member. Such leadership is facilitative rather than restrictive in regard to the group's area of freedom.

A democratic style of leadership is based on the belief that the collective wisdom is greater than that of any single member. In the words of Thomas Jefferson: "I know of no safe depository of the ultimate powers of society but the people themselves."[9] Fundamental to democratic leadership is the belief that all persons affected by a decision should have a voice in making the decision. In a democratic climate, any attempt to coerce or manipulate is both immoral and impractical. Immoral because manipulation destroys the human capacity

---

[9]Saul Padover (ed.), *Thomas Jefferson on Democracy* (New York: Appleton-Century, 1939), p. 162.

to reason and decide for one's self. Impractical because manipulation when sensed leads to apathy, resistance or even counterforce. A democratic leader participates with the group in making decisions concerning both the procedure and substance of discussions. He serves the group rather than making it his servant.

In practice, a democratic discussion leader will suggest procedures, but he will not impose them. He may suggest a plan or solution, but will be quite ready to follow any procedure or accept any solution which the group, by consensus, prefers. For example, he will say, "What do you think about . . . ," rather than, "We will . . . ."

Both autocratic and democratic styles of discussion leadership are in stark contrast to what is often called a laissez-faire style. It is not leadership, but an abdication of responsibility for leading. The laissez-faire leader does virtually nothing. He comes to meetings unprepared. In practice, he may open a discussion by saying: "It's about time we started our discussion." He then sits back, exerts no influence, does virtually nothing to organize, clarify or promote a solution. Into the void someone must step, or the group will flounder aimlessly. When a group first meets, the usual result is either anarchy or a struggle for status. A group of skilled discussants, given this kind of leader, may proceed fairly well, but all too often they waste time or else an autocrat takes over. Apathy and frustration are common.

Many times a designated discussion leader is in a bureaucratic position as part of a larger organization; he may need to exert bureaucratic leadership. For example, a foreman is charged by his superiors with seeing that certain tasks are accomplished by the work group. A study-discussion leader is partly responsible to the organization sponsoring the study-discussion program (often a university, public library or great books foundation). The chairman of a committee appointed to carry out a task or to make recommendations is responsible to the parent body. A department head is bound by regulations and responsibilities which he cannot ignore. Such a bureaucratic leader must blend autocratic and democratic styles, making clear the area of freedom of the group, and the limits placed on him and the group. Some of the topics to be discussed, the procedures to be followed during discussion, and specific recommendations or solutions to be applied can be determined by the group as a whole.

A major problem is that the *position of leader* and *leadership* are likely to be confused. Teachers and experts who seek to be as democratic as possible often find themselves in such a dilemma. A teacher who seeks to develop members of his class by having them determine the organization of a course, or plan projects and assignments will often find the class trying to force him into an autocratic role by being overly submissive and eagerly acquiescent to his every suggestion.

A remedy may be to adopt a nondirective style of leading which puts responsibility on the group for directing their activities. The leader must exercise great self-control, withholding leadership at critical junctures, even letting the group flounder at times, so that participants will develop their own skills and motives. The nondirective leader will call attention to problems facing the group, whether of task or group maintenance, but he will not solve them. On some occasions he may suggest and invite other alternatives, but he will still leave the decision to the group. This is not an abdication of leadership. Whereas the laissez-faire leader does nothing, a nondirective leader works very hard at his job. He listens intently. He reflects his observations back to the group. He may clarify a problem, supply information, or summarize what he has noticed, but he always asks the group if they agree. He will ask many questions and will rebound to the group questions calling for his judgment or opinion. In time he will find he can lead democratically and still discharge his responsibilities to a superior or parent body by making clear to all group members what must be done. Once members are accustomed to accepting responsibility for making decisions which affect them, they will not want it any other way. Apathy will virtually disappear if the goals are truly group goals.

FUNCTIONS AND RESPONSIBILITIES OF THE DISCUSSION LEADER

A designated discussion leader cannot evade the responsibility for certain tasks and functions. Most adults are members of many small groups, and have neither the time nor the resources available to keep abreast of all details, regulations and changes in the groups. Often we come rushing into a meeting, literally out of breath, with our minds still occupied by other matters. In this condition we try to orient ourselves to another discussion. If our leaders (or teachers) greet us with, "Well, what shall we do today?" we are likely to be irritated and to get nothing done. Students with five classes a day and businessmen with a dozen conferences a day must place special responsibilities on designated discussion leaders. The leader in such cases has a special job to do, and doing it well will foster democracy. The group still retains the power to decide within its area of freedom, and can act more wisely because the leader has served it well.

The discussion leader must decide on an approach to his tasks. He must decide on the *quantity and kind of control* he will exercise. There are times when strict control over certain matters is necessary. Limits imposed by a parent organization must be strictly observed. Considerable control of the group process may be necessary. When working with peers, many leaders err because of too little control. When rank, status or age creates a gulf between a designated leader and the rest of the group, the tendency is to exert too much control. Each designated discussion leader must decide his own course, but he should be constantly reviewing it for needed changes. In short, he must experiment to find out what most helps a particular group achieve its goals.

Normally, it is necessary to exert more control on procedures in the early part of a discussion or in the early life of a group than later. It is *wiser to supply too much procedural control than too little.* Once initial order has been established it is easy to relax controls. To bring order out of chaos is most difficut. A few guidelines may help the designated leader determine what to do:

1. *Group expectations* should be determined and adapted to. At least initially, a group leader will need to conform to what the members expect in his role.

2. *Group purpose* affects leader control. Learning, cathartic or value-sharing groups usually need far less structure and control than groups facing complex problems.

3. *Group methods* vary in the amount of control needed. Brainstorming or buzz group procedures in a classroom require strict procedural control, whereas a less complex pattern for organizing group thinking will take far less procedural control from a designated leader.

4. *Membership skills and maturity* must be taken into account. Members with training and experience in discussion are much more able to share in leadership than are members with little or no training in discussion techniques.

5. *The leader's skill and confidence* should determine how he acts. It is decidedly more difficult to share tasks of procedural leadership than to monopolize them. Democratic leadership calls for skills in listening, organizing, summarizing and timing that may take a long time to develop.

6. *Time urgency* may be a factor. Occasionally a decision must be made in a hurry, in which case a group will welcome strict control on its procedures. When time is not limited and members are vitally affected by what they decide, they will need little control.

7. *Highly involved groups require less control.* When members perceive the task as important to them personally, they will often resent any domination. The implication is clear: The designated discussion leader should see that all members realize the importance of the task; he must get them involved and concerned.

This brings us to the specific functions of the designated discussion leader, and ways in which he may perform them well. Any of these functions can be performed by any member, but the designated leader has the special responsibility to see that they are done. He should do them only to the degree necessary for efficiency and group cohesiveness. First, we will consider functions and responsibilities which may fall on any discussion leader, followed by tasks needed only in special types of discussions.

General Functions of Discussion Leaders

Planning and preparation. Planning and preparation for discussion have been discussed in Chapter 3 in detail. Designated discussion leaders have special responsibilities for the tasks described there: gathering information, agenda preparation, drawing up tentative outlines for guiding group thinking, notifying members of meetings, and having all physical facilities ready. Additional leadership functions can be classified into four categories: guiding, stimulating thinking, facilitating communication, promoting cooperative interpersonal relations, and developing the group and its members.

Guiding

A. Initiate the discussion.
　1. Keep opening remarks as brief as possible.
　2. See that all members are acquainted with each other and put at ease. A brief coffee hour may permit you to do this. Use name cards for a new group.
　3. Announce the topic or purpose of the discussion and its importance. Make sure the area of freedom is clear to all.
　4. Distribute any fact sheets or other materials that will be needed.
　5. Attempt to establish an informal atmosphere in which members feel secure, yet feel responsible enough to contribute.
　6. Announce any rules of procedure. You may want the group to set these up, but be prepared to suggest procedures.
　7. Suggest an outline for group thinking and get the group to accept or modify it.
　8. If needed, get a group recorder. If any other special leadership services are needed, see that someone is prepared to supply them.

B. Keep the discussion orderly and organized.
　1. Once the group has adopted an outline or plan to guide its thinking, it can be put on a chalkboard or chart.
　2. Keep the group oriented toward its goal. Be sure the goal is clearly understood by all and is the goal toward which the

group wants to move. From time to time you may need to ask, "How will this help us achieve our purposes?" or "Are we losing sight of our objectives?" When asked to do so, discussants frequently write down very different statements of the group's objectives!

3. Watch for any extended digressions. When you notice one, you can point it out and ask the group what to do about it. If a discussant offers a solution prematurely, you might ask him to hold it until the group has finished "mapping" the problem. If someone changes topics in a learning discussion, you might ask if the group has finished with the previous topic.

4. In a problem-solving discussion, see that all findings, ideas, criteria and possible solutions are accurately recorded.

5. If you notice a lot of repeating with nothing new being added, ask if the group is ready for the next topic.

6. Summarize, or see that a summary is made of each major part of the discussion. Be sure the summary is complete and acceptable to the entire group. Sometimes a summary can be made by reviewing what is on the chart or board.

7. Make a clear transition to each new question or step. This can be combined with a summary. For example, "We have found that time pressures, high cost of duplication, and lack of policing contribute to theft and mutilation. Are we ready to consider possible solutions? (pause) Okay, what might we do to reduce theft and mutilation?"

8. See that all major topics or phases of problem solving are thoroughly discussed. Point out anything of importance that is being overlooked.

9. Keep track of time, and remind the group of any time limits so they can consider all aspects of the problem.

10. Bring the discussion to a definite conclusion. Too often a discussion ends without any sense of closure. Members suddenly remember they have to be elsewhere, and dash off amid chaos. Any plan for the future is left unfinished. The conclusion might include any or all of the following: a summary of all progress made by the group; a statement of how reports of the meeting will be distributed to members and other interested persons; comments about preparations for the next meeting; assignments for follow-up and implementation; commendations to the group for a job well done; an evaluation of the meeting to improve the group's future discussions (Chapter 8 discusses in detail how to do this).

C. Encourage participation by all members.
1. See that all members have an equal chance to participate. While no one should be forced to speak, neither should anyone be prevented from speaking by other members.
2. Address your comments and questions to the group, not to individuals, unless you want to elicit a specific bit of information.
3. Point out in the beginning of the discussion that you will be primarily a procedural leader, that you will not offer personal opinions, and that the substance of the discussion must come from the group as a whole.
4. Make a visual survey of all members every minute or two, looking for any indication that a member may want to speak. If you see such a reaction from a discussant who has had little to say, "gatekeep" him into the discussion by saying something like, "Joe, did you want to comment on that idea?" Encourage him to speak, but do not embarrass him if he has nothing to say by asking a question like, "Joe, what do you think about that idea?"
5. If the group contains compulsive talkers who make long speeches or who speak so often that others get little chance, try to control them for the benefit of the group.

   The following techniques may help:

   When you ask a question of the group, let your eyes meet those of members who have spoken infrequently and avoid those of highly vocal members.

   When a compulsive talker has made a point, cut in with, "How do the rest of you feel about that idea?"

   Restate briefly what has been said at length.

   Ask each person to make only one point per speech.

   Have one member keep a count of frequency of participation, then report his findings to the group.

   Point out the problem and ask others to contribute more. For instance, "We have heard a lot from Peter and Marion, but what do the rest of you think about . . .?"

   In private, ask the frequent talkers to help you get the quiet members to speak more often.

   Seat talkative members where you can easily overlook them.
6. Rebound questions to the group, unless you are the only person who can answer. If a member asks for your opinion, you might reply: "Well, let's see how other group members feel about this."

7. Speak only when necessary. Don't comment after each member has spoken.
8. React with acceptance and without evaluation, showing only that you understand or need clarification. If evaluation seems necessary, invite it from others with a question such as, "How well does that agree with other information we have?"
9. React silently. It is important for you to nod or otherwise show you heard and understood, especially when an infrequent participant speaks.

Stimulate both Creative and Critical Thinking

It has already been pointed out that creative and critical thinking do not mix well. However, someone must ask questions at appropriate times to spark imagination or to promote critical thinking by group members. A hypercritical atmosphere may stop the flow of information and ideas, or a sweetness-and-light atmosphere may develop in which nobody feels free to challenge faulty evidence or ideas.

To encourage critical thinking, try the following techniques:
1. Keep asking for information and analysis of the problem if the group gets solution minded.
2. See that evidence is tested for reliability and not accepted at face value. You might do this by asking questions which will encourage the group members to test and evaluate it. For example:

    To check the relevance of evidence, you might ask, "How does this apply to our problem?" or "How is that like the situation we are discussing?"

    To evaluate the source of evidence, you might ask such questions as, "What is the source of that information?" "How well is _____ recognized in his field?" "Is this consistent with his other pronouncements on the subject?"

    To check on the credibility of information, you might ask: "Do we have any information which is contradictory?"

    To test a statistic, you might ask how it was derived or how an average was computed.

3. See that all group members understand and evaluate all standards, criteria or assumptions used in making value judgments. For example, you might ask, "Is that criterion clear to us all?" "Is this something we want to insist upon?" or "Do we all accept that as an assumption?"
4. See that all proposed solutions are given a thorough testing before they are accepted as group decisions. Encourage the group to apply the available facts and all the criteria. Some questions you might ask:

"Do we have any evidence to indicate that this solution would be satisfactory? Unsatisfactory?"

"Are there any facts to support this proposal?"

"How well would this idea meet our criteria?"

"Would that proposal get at the basic problem?"

"Is there any way we can test this idea before we decide whether or not to adopt it?"

Encouraging creative thinking is equally important. The description of the problem is an especially rich source of ideas, so keep the group on the problem until it has been thoroughly described. A few special techniques:

1. Apply the principle of deferred judgment even when not brainstorming, and try to get as many alternative solutions as possible. Perhaps you can use some of the following questions:

   "How *might* we . . .?" (rather than "How *should* we . . .?")

   "What other ideas can we think of?"

   "Can we recall any solutions used elsewhere that might be used to help solve this problem?"

2. An effective device is to take up each major characteristic of the problem and ask how it might be modified, solved or eliminated.
3. Watch for possible solutions which suggest whole new areas of thinking, and then pose a general question about the new area. For example, if a member suggests signs in the library to warn about the cost of theft, you might ask, "How else might we publicize the cost of losses to the library?

Promote Clear Communication

A designated discussion leader has a great opportunity to serve as a model of effective listening. Only when discussants listen to understand each other can they think together. Occasional summarizing will help promote understanding and clear communication, but there is much more the leader can do.

Try to reduce the expression of ideas and judgments in biased, loaded or emotive language. Aside from being a model, you can often rephrase or question a biased statement. For example:

Member: "Such socialistic ideas will ruin our country."

Leader: "You feel that governmental control would somehow do more harm than good. How do the others feel about this?"

Member: "The cops are brutal to Negroes."

Leader: "You believe that the police use undue force when arresting a Negro? What evidence do you have that this is so?"

Whenever a statement is unclear to you or when you see a discussant showing signs of not listening or of being confused (such as a frown or puzzled look), check for understanding. You might say something like, "I'm not sure I understand that. Do the rest of you?" "Let me see if I got your meaning. I think you said that . . ." "I'm not sure we all understood your point. Could you give us some examples, or describe how it would work?" "Joe, you seem puzzled by what Marcia said." "Is that point clear to us all?" Especially watch for minority points of view, and insist that they should be at least understood by all participants. Novel and unusual ideas are often ignored or rejected without being considered.

Promote Cooperative Interpersonal Relations

Many things can interfere with the ability of members to cooperate with each other. An important responsibility of leadership is sensing the climate of interpersonal relations and member feelings, then doing whatever may be needed to promote satisfaction and harmony within a group. Clear communication, acceptance, orderly procedures and a sense of accomplishment will do much to promote good interpersonal relations and cohesiveness. However, discussion is not an entirely rational and logical process. People have feelings and are motivated for many different reasons. The designated leader can do many things which may help bring unity out of a conflict over values or ideas:

1. Watch for indications of hidden agendas at variance with the group objectives. Call these to the attention of the group. The group can usually solve a problem of conflicting purposes if the members are fully aware of it.
2. Emphasize the importance of seeking only mutually acceptable solutions. Stress the unity of purpose which brought the group into existence by using the word *we* often.
3. Keep conflicts focused on facts and issues, stopping at once any attacks on a member's personality or character.
4. Don't let the discussion get so serious that people cannot enjoy themselves. Humor may help reduce the tensions that are generated when people work hard together at the job of hammering out ideas. Good task leaders may have trouble with humor. Lee observed that many of the most efficient discussion leaders were lacking in human warmth.

When men are driven, they lose spontaneity and the zestful interest in what goes on. . . . There is a very real danger that our concern with improving human communication may lead members to forget the human part of the matter. . . . We need efficiency *and* satisfyingness. One may try to rig a discussion in the image of a belt line; if he succeeds he may find that those who attend become as inert as machines without the capacity (or will) to create.

[To maintain a balance in discussion, Lee suggested that designated leaders] listen with lessened tension when the bent to comedy or diversion or personal release is being manifested . . . [and] pick up the problem *after* the camaraderie or tension has been spent.[10]

Tensions build, and they must be released or interpersonal friction will grow. Effective discussion is characterized by a constant shifting between the serious and the playful, the relevant and the remote, kidding and criticism. The result of such tension-relieving activity is much more concerted action by group members. If you are not skilled at relieving tensions, welcome the leadership of members who are.

5. When a group seems to be deadlocked, look for a basis on which to compromise. Conferees may represent points of view which they cannot abandon or sell out, but eventually a decision must be made. For example, labor and management negotiators must eventually agree on a contract if the company is to work. To handle the problems presented by conferees representing diverse interests, we can use techniques employed by mediators of bargaining conferences. The mediator seeks to find a common ground, a *compromise* solution which all parties can accept as the *best achievable solution.* Each partisan yields something in order to obtain something. In common parlance, "half a loaf is better than none." A complete surrender by one of two or more partisans will only postpone the settlement of a basic issue.

To encourage compromise, you may first need to point out that compromise need not be a sellout or dirty word. As Edmund Burke put it, "All government, — indeed every human benefit and enjoyment, every virtue and every prudent act, — is founded on compromise and barter."[11] Second, insist that the interests and needs of each participant are clearly understood by all other participants. Find the minimum conditions which are acceptable to every conferee, and then suggest a solution which will meet these minimums. Of course, this may take a great deal of discussion. By this pro-

[10]Irving J. Lee, *How to Talk with People* (New York: Harper and Brothers, 1952), pp. 158-160.
[11]*Ibid.*, pp. 90-91.

cedure a group may substitute intelligence and cooperation for the good of all in place of conflict and harm for all.

Develop the Group and Its Members

The need for personal and group development will vary widely from person to person and group to group. A continuing group, such as a college class, a standing committee, an engineering staff, or a study-discussion group should definitely allow time for feedback and evaluation of meetings. A one-meeting discussion group, on the other hand, may have no reason to spend time evaluating the group processes.

Sometimes the impetus for growth can be given by asking the group, after a discussion has ended, to examine its discussion. For example, a designated leader might ask, "How did we do in our discussion?" or "What might we do to make our next meeting more profitable than this one?" If a group is having trouble, the leader might interrupt the discussion with some comment such as this: "We seem to be making little headway. What's wrong? How might we get more accomplished (or, relieve this tension, or make the discussion more interesting)?" The specific question should be in reaction to what he senses is wrong.

A class studying discussion techniques should have at least one observer for every discussion. The observer may break into the conversation to point out what he sees is hampering the group, make a brief report after the discussion, fill out rating forms which the group can discuss, or raise questions pertinent to the group's procedures. Any continuing group will benefit by doing this occasionally; any member can serve the group as an observer if he refrains from regular participation. However it is done, a definite leadership service is made to a continuing group when members are made more aware of how they are participating and interacting together. In Chapter 8 the role of observer and procedures for group evaluation are explained in detail.

The preceding list of leadership functions and techniques is at best a partial one. Whatever his techniques, the leader must be flexible, adapting to the specific group. The main tools of the discussion leader are carefully laid plans, questions, skillful listening, clarifying comments, effective summarizing, tension-relieving humor and appropriate observations which are fed back to the entire group. Democratic, shared leadership, even when one person has been designated the leader, contributes most to group success and member development.

BIBLIOGRAPHY

Haiman, Franklyn S., *Group Leadership and Democratic Action*, Boston: Houghton Mifflin Company, 1951.

Lee, Irving J., *How to Talk with People,* New York: Harper and Brothers, 1952.

Maier, Norman R. F., *Problem-solving Discussions and Conferences,* New York: McGraw-Hill Book Company, 1963.

Tannenbaum, Robert, Weschler, Irving R., and Massarik, Fred, *Leadership and Organization: A Behavioral Science Approach,* New York: McGraw-Hill Book Company, 1961.

EXERCISES

1. Select a case problem, preferably from your own experience, for which you do not have a solution. Prepare and distribute copies to all members of your discussion group. During the discussion a classmate should serve as observer, rating you as a leader. Following the discussion (20-30 minutes as assigned by your instructor), the observer will guide your group in a brief evaluation of the discussion. At the class meeting after the discussion you should hand the following to your instructor: (1) a copy of the case; (2) a copy of your leader's outline; (3) a report of the discussion following the format on page 50; (4) the observer's rating sheet evaluating your leadership; (5) a brief essay in which you evaluate your functioning as leader of the discussion.

2. Select a short poem and make copies to distribute to half of your class. Then conduct a discussion of this poem. Two or more groups may be discussing simultaneously, each with one or more observers.

3. Buzz groups should draw up lists of topics, problems or value questions about which all members would like to learn more. Select the subject of most interest to the group, and compile a bibliography of pertinent materials. Each discussant should then do the required reading, making study notes and a tentative leader's outline. Then the group can discuss the topic, with the designated leadership rotating every fifteen to twenty minutes. One or more observers should report their findings before each new designated leader takes on his responsibilities. Some possible questions:

   "How important is religious activity to a college student?"

   "What should be the role of government in higher education?"

   "What should be our national policy toward abortion?"

4. Select a problem. Then have each class member prepare and deliver a leader's opening remarks for initiating a discussion of the problem. Have the class evaluate each introduction.

5. After a brief discussion, have each participant write a summary of what was said. Compare the summaries. What can you conclude?

6. Plan and conduct a panel discussion, based on previous closed-group discussions in class. While one group is presenting its panel, the rest of the class will serve as an audience. The entire class can then evaluate the moderator's techniques, the organization of the discussion, the spread of time and participation among the participants, and the handling of the forum following the panel discussion.

7. Role play some problem-solving discussions (preferably using case problems presented by your instructor). Two or three problem members should be planted in each group, doing such things as pleading personal interests, sidetracking and introducing irrelevant issues, making cutting personal criticisms, talking incessantly, remaining silent and so forth. Experiment with various leader techniques for handling these problem members and evaluate the results.

Chapter 6

PARTICIPATING
EFFECTIVELY

While much of what was said about effective leadership could be repeated in a chapter on participating, no one can lead well without having good followers. Participating refers to being active, verbally or otherwise, in group interaction. In this chapter we will look at the attitudes and activities of the ideal group member who is not designated as a leader.

ATTITUDES OF AN IDEAL DISCUSSANT

Responsibility to the Group

A whole set of attitudes can be summarized in the one phrase *a sense of responsibility for the success of the group.* The effective discussant feels a personal responsibility to see that the group achieves its goals, and will do all he can to help. He cannot "let George do it" or say, "it's their fault" when success is not achieved.

During a discussion he feels a responsibility to participate actively. He offers what he can, and at least shows his reactions to the thoughts of others. He feels that the group needs to be aware of the ideas and judgments of every member.

This responsibility to the group continues after the discussion. The ideal discussant supports the group decisions. He speaks of "we" rather than "I" and "they." He accepts a full share of the blame for any group failure, and no more than his share of credit for group success. He carries out any task which he accepted as a representative of the group, never accepting any responsibility which he cannot or will not discharge. He respects the confidence and trust of other group members, not revealing what they have stated in confidence during a discussion.

Objectivity in Acceptance of Ideas

An ideal discussant displays an attitude of scientific objectivity toward the subject of discussion. He realizes that all knowledge is subject to the frailties of the human observers from whom it came. He is aware that we do not know everything about anything, so he maintains a mood of open-minded inquiry, seeking further information from other group members. Such a participant is willing to change his interpretations, beliefs or values in the light of new information. He not only listens patiently to a new or different point of view; he does so eagerly.

While the good discussant is open-minded, he is no spineless weathervane, shifting to conform to each new idea or point of view. On the contrary, he can make up his mind and support an idea, but only so far as it is supported by evidence and reasoning.

But if a discussant's view of communication is that it is a process of changing or persuading others to accept his views, clash is inevitable and cooperation is possible only if someone *gives in* (notice the language of combat and conflict). If discussants begin with the assumption that the purpose of communicating in a discussion group is to achieve understanding of each other's points of view, beliefs and information, then *voluntary change* and *cooperation* are possible. Only the person who has freely and voluntarily changed his mind will be a strong supporter of his new point of view. As Alexander Pope said in his *Essay on Man*:

> A man convinced against his will
> Is of the same opinion still.

Objectivity in Acceptance of Other Members

Attitudes toward other individuals in a group are affected by attitudes toward information and ideas and toward self. If we feel insecure, we tend to see the rest of the members of a group as threatening and hostile. If we believe we know all that needs to be known, or that our ideas are the right ones, we see other persons as stupid, misinformed, illogical, dishonest, close-minded or bullheaded. Such is the mechanism of projection, whereby we see in others the weaknesses in our own persons.

Acceptance of others is essential to cooperating with them. If you reject the person because you do not like his looks, conduct, race or idea, he is likely to reject you. "Condemn not that ye be not condemned" is a sound motto in human relations. Some people seem to be often in a blaming or condemning mood; such people cannot work well with others. If a participant in a discussion group focuses on motives and personalities rather than on what other discussants *say* and the *goals* of the group, he can only expect a lack of trust and group achievement. Psychologizing should be left to the professionals.

Two productive assumptions about other group members are that they want to achieve the best possible solutions, and that they are reasonable people. These assumptions lead one to focus on the substance and process of the discussion, to view information and ideas objectively rather than attacking the motives and character of the source. People tend to be what we make of them. If we show, by word or manner, that we trust, then they tend to be trustworthy. If we show respect for their reasonableness, they tend to be reasonable. Doubtless you have noticed that professors who expect students to cheat will have much more cheating than will professors who show that they expect students to be honest. Granted there are some unscrupulous, self-seeking people in discussion groups. You can maintain the guard of testing evidence and ideas by impersonal, standard criteria.

Whenever a member of a group loses face he is likely to create a serious problem. He may withdraw, become aggressive toward others or balk at any change. Cooperation between people is possible only if they give each other mutual respect and goodwill. Not everyone's ideas are equally worthy, but everyone's ideas are equally worthy of attention. Everyone deserves to have his questions answered without sarcasm and to have his suggestions accorded respectful consideration.

Objective evaluation of other members' ideas is as important as acceptance. Discussants should guard against the halo effect, by which we tend to perceive what another says or does on the basis of some general impression of his status. Because we like a man we may accept his ideas uncritically. Because he is highly fluent he does not necessarily have dependable information nor is his summary necessarily accurate. A person who has invented one excellent idea may produce a dud the next time. High esteem or expertise of a speaker in one subject should not lower our critical testing of ideas when he talks on another subject. It has been suggested that we should view all experts and great men as if they were in their underwear — at least that should help us maintain a high degree of objectivity toward their ideas! Goodwill, friendship, trust and respect for the person *as a person* must not cloud our thinking or lower our objectivity in evaluating information and ideas. The author often has students sign a card which reads: "I understand that I do not have to believe a single thing I hear the instructor say nor a single thing I read in connection with this course." As group members, we need the objectivity this card is intended to foster.

A particular danger of status differences is that high status persons tend to ignore or reject ideas from persons of lower status. Low status persons tend to accept or reject uncritically the ideas of high status persons. In the one case, the low status person accepts an authority figure uncritcially; in the other, he acts defensively. To help assure that all discussants will be given an equitable hearing, it is helpful to have all addressed in a similar manner, for instance, by first names, titles or "Mr.," "Mrs.," and "Miss."

Objectivity in Acceptance of Self

Before one can act with acceptance and respect toward others, he must first accept and respect himself. As Shakespeare said, "To thine own self be true, and it must follow as the day the night, thou canst not be untrue to any man." If you have doubts about your competence, prepare thoroughly rather than falling into the trap of being either arrogant or acquiescent. If you speak hesitantly and without enthusiasm, others are likely to hesitate to accept what you say. Before you can be an effective discussant you will have to correct any serious misgivings about yourself. The best advice is to prepare yourself well, present your ideas and see what happens.

Self-satisfaction can be as harmful as self-rejection. A person who is not constantly examining his own behavior will grow and learn very little. Notice how others are reacting to you. Listen to yourself — how do you sound? Were you a source of sidetracking or did you help the group maintain direction? Did you contribute all you might have or did you withhold information and ideas which might have helped the group? A useful practice is to occasionally listen to a recording of yourself in a discussion, applying all the criteria to yourself that you could apply to any other person. Helpful, also, is a feedback session such as is described in the final chapter of this book. If you get the opportunity to do so, participate in a group training laboratory, "T-group" or sensitivity training group. Objectivity and respect for every group member is the goal — and that includes yourself.

SKILLS OF AN IDEAL DISCUSSANT

While the attitudes discussed in the previous section are pre-requisites to being an effective discussant, there are many specific skills you can learn which will also make you a more effective discussant. These concern *what* you contribute, *when* you contribute and how you contribute.

He Communicates Effectively

Communicate Openly

The effective discussant reacts so that others can be constantly aware of his state of mind. There is nothing so depressing as a group of people sitting like zombies while another is speaking. Response and reaction are essential to cooperative thinking and good interpersonal relations. When you agree, show it with a nod or verbal assent. When you disagree, show it. When you have a question, ask it. When you have a feeling of warmth for others, communicate it with a word, smile or gesture. Nothing is quite so inconsiderate of another as to ignore him; lack of response, at least from the other person's point of view, is ignoring.

Speak Effectively

Desire to communicate. The speaker who drones without emphasis or who speaks with so little force that he can barely be heard really does not care about his listeners. He is thinking aloud, speaking to himself. Think of your speaking in relation to a scale ranging from "trying hard, wanting to be heard and believed" to "an air of not trying and not caring to be understood." Where do you fall on such a scale? If you fall near the "not caring" end, ask yourself why you sound like this. Maybe you don't care. If so, don't discuss.[1]

Speak to the group. To keep the channels for participation open to all, address your remarks to the entire group. You may begin a response to an individual, but extend your eye contact to include all members. Speaking to a chairman especially restricts spontaneity and effectiveness of group thinking. What you say should be of interest to everyone, and everyone should be made to feel equally free to respond.

Organize your remarks. A useful comment does not come at random, nor is it randomly expressed. A general pattern to follow is this: relate the contribution to what has already been said by another; state the idea; develop and support it; connect the contribution to the topic or phase of the problem being discussed. You will notice that this format provides an answer to the three basic questions to be asked when evaluating any extended contribution: What is the point? How do you know? How does it matter at this time? For example:

---

[1]Lee, *op. cit.*, p. 124. Lee reports that observers can use such a scale with considerable agreement. It would be instructive to rate all of your classmates on such a scale.

Helen, you said many magazine articles have been cut out. I also found that every encyclopedia had articles removed from it. The librarian told me that it costs about $1,000.00 per year to replace damaged encyclopedias. So we can see that a serious part of the problem is the loss of widely used reference materials.

State one point at a time. This is not an inviolable rule, but generally speaking, you should not contribute more than one idea in a single speech. A several-point speech is definitely out. A group can discuss only one idea at a time; confusion is likely to result if you try to make several points at once. A comment in which you attempt to give all the data on an issue or present a series of points is likely to be too involved to be grasped and responded to.

Speak concisely. If listeners appear bored or restive, you have spoken at too great length. Try to state your ideas as simply and briefly as possible. Some participants restate every point several times, or take two hundred words to say what could be stated in twenty. This reduces the opportunity for others to participate, and often results in the long speech being tuned out by others.

Use appropriate language. Vague, general words often lead to misunderstanding. Language that is not a part of the vocabulary of the group members will help no one. The purpose is not to display your erudition, but to contribute to group understanding. Concrete instances or examples, an analogy relating a new idea to a familiar one, or a vivid description are just as important in discussion as in public speaking.

Don't Monopolize

You should, of course, enter the discussion whenever you have anything new, relevant and useful to offer. But watch to see that you are not monopolizing time or discouraging others from participating. Remember that the larger the group, the greater the probability that a few members will over participate.

He Helps Maintain Order and Organization

The ideal discussant shares in the responsibility for procedural leadership, if only by following the pattern and procedures agreed on by the group. If he feels a change in group procedure or topic is needed, he makes this known. But he then acts in concert with the majority, whether or not they accept his proposed change. In addition, he relates all comments to the previous remarks and the issue under consideration. When he notices the group getting off track or losing sight of its goals, he points this out. For example, he might say, "We were trying to plan a picnic, but now we are talking about a riot. Haven't we forgotten our purpose?"

He Listens to Understand

Effective listening is an active process, requiring as much effort as speaking. Unless we listen closely, we will not have all the information needed to make sound decisions. Often several discussants in turn say almost the same thing, as if they had never heard what the first person said. This wastes time; it can be prevented by listening closely to others instead of thinking about what we will say next.

It is especially important to listen to understand the other person's meaning before reacting. The sidetracking and irrelevancy which result from half listening are costly of time and goodwill. A good test of your listening is to restate, in your own words, the meaning of the previous speaker. The author's discussion classes often do this as an exercise to develop effective listening during discussion. Each discussant is required to restate the prior speaker's ideas to the person's satisfaction. If the restatement is not accepted as accurate, then the new speaker loses the floor. In many groups, more than fifty per cent of the restatements are rejected as being inaccurate or incomplete. If misunderstanding is so common even when great effort to understand is being made, how common must it be in ordinary discussions?

Only when you are sure you understand another person's point of view should you evaluate his comment. Then critical listening is in order. Was his comment pertinent? Is there a basis in evidence and experience for what he said? Is his statement logically valid? Does he present a biased picture of events? Good listening, then, is a process of understanding what another meant from his point of view, then evaluating the significance and dependability of his comments.

He Maintains Perspective

Perspective is needed on the expenditure of time. Some impatient discussants expect a group to move to a conclusion as rapidly as an individual. These people show no tolerance for the time-consuming process of talking out an idea until it is understood by all members. They want immediate solutions rather than mutually acceptable ones, not realizing that hasty decisions may have to be made all over again because differences in belief were suppressed. Men are not computers. Only men can solve new and important problems. And only men can interpret the breakdowns in understanding involved in social upheaval. Time spent in achieving understanding and mutually acceptable solutions is an investment in future efficiency. On the other hand, time wasted on irrelevancies, on interpersonal conflicts, on rambling speeches or on misunderstandings due to poor listening is time lost forever.

Perspective is needed on group norms: What are they, what are they producing? In some discussion groups profanity is permitted, in others it is taboo. Some groups are very formal, while others are relaxed and casual. The effective discussant makes it his business to detect the norms of his group and adapt to them. Later, if he feels they are handicapping the group or some of its members, he can bring the norm to the attention of the group, point out what he feels is wrong with it and suggest an alternative. But only a person lacking in perspective on his group role would make an immediate frontal assault on norms and values long accepted by other members.

Perspective is needed on the power to produce conformity. Many studies have demonstrated that a group can exert great pressure on its members to conform in judgment, belief and action. Summarizing these studies, Hare concluded that a group member is likely to change an opinion *"when the object to be judged is ambiguous,* if he must make his *opinion public,* if the *majority holding a contrary opinion is large,* and if the *group is especially friendly or close knit."*[2] All of these conditions are likely to be found in a continuing discussion group.

There is much you can do to reduce conformity of opinions. First, if members are made aware of the pressure to conform they can resist it more successfully. Support from one other person, especially a designated discussion leader, is often sufficient to help a person maintain a point of view until the idea has been tested on its own merits. It is even possible to establish a group norm of considering all minority points of view before reaching a decision. Certainly we need the kind of perspective that comes from remembering that every new idea in the world was at its inception in a minority of one and that fifty million Frenchmen can be wrong.

Finally, we need perspective when one of our pet ideas has been rejected. The ideal discussant realizes that even though his evidence and inferences are rejected, he as a person is not rejected. He can and should continue to do everything possible to help the group reach the best possible solution, and then support the final group decision.

In this chapter effective participation has been described as resulting from attitudes of responsibility, objective acceptance of new ideas and information, objective acceptance of other members and objective acceptance of self. If he has these attitudes, a person will be an effective discussant to the degree that he communicates openly,

---

[2]A. Paul Hare, *Handbook of Small Group Research* (New York: The Free Press of Glencoe, 1962), pp. 30-31.

speaks effectively, helps maintain order and listens to understand. Finally, while discussing he must maintain perspective regarding the use of time, the effects of group norms, the pressures to conform to majority opinions and the merits of his own ideas.

Chapter 7

IMPROVING COMMUNICATION IN DISCUSSIONS

"What we need in this outfit is better communications." "The most important thing in running a business is good communications." Such frequently repeated statements indicate we live in a communication conscious world. But while most of us are concerned, few of us are aware of what goes wrong when men attempt to communicate or what to do when it does.

Communication refers to the entire process by which one person evokes meaning in another. Communication may be intentional, accidental or both; it may be oral, gestural or both; it may be verbal, non-verbal or both. Leaving aside the subject of moral responsibility in communicating, we can say that intentional (or purposive) communication is effective to the degree that the receiver responds in the way intended by the sender. Even though I want to appear calm, I may accidentally communicate tension by jiggling my pencil, twisting in my chair or straining my voice. I may intend to communicate an image of how to seat a panel group in a television studio, but your resultant understanding may be such that you get the arrangement all fouled up. As the subjects of discussion become more complex, the likelihood of miscommunication increases rapidly. Since discussion groups do not deal with the purely factual or the cut and dried, the probability of misunderstanding among discussants is very great.

This chapter will first explore some of the more common types of communication breakdowns which occur during discussion and some things we can do to prevent or alleviate them. Second, it considers how questions can help or hinder communication in a discussion group. Suggestions made in earlier chapters for improving communication will not be repeated. The general subject of speech communication is explored thoroughly in other books, which you would be wise to study if you have not already done so.

SOME BREAKDOWNS AND CORRECTIVES

By-Passing

Each of us has a *selective filter system* which admits some parts of a communication stimulus, rejects other parts and distorts still others. Miscommunication which stems from such differing perceptions is called *by-passing*. Two people are by-passing when they assume each has approximately the same image or idea in mind as the other, but the images are actually quite different. They are "talking past each other."

By-passing is based on two fundamental fallacies about language. The first of these fallacies, called the "container myth," is that *words have meaning* in and of themselves. If a word contains meaning and I give you the right word, you are bound to get the right meaning. But there is no intrinsic connection between any word and any thing, experience or relationship. Words are symbols for experience, representing whatever we choose to have them represent. *Meaning resides in the user of the word,* not in the word (or phrase or sentence). If by agreement or conventional usage two people use the same word to refer to the same type of thing, then they can communicate adequately. But the persons attempting to communicate must discover whether or not their meanings are sufficiently similar before they can know what has been communicated.

The second fallacy is that *words have monousage.* This assumption is patently ridiculous, but we often act as if it were valid. For example, the author once listened to twenty minutes of by-passing during a discussion on religion. One man stated that man lacked free will. Another man avowed that man did have free will. Other members took sides, and the argument raged. To the author, a nonparticipant, it appeared that both sides believed that man could make limited choices, but what he chose was in large part determined by his past experiences. Several members of the group also became aware of the basic agreement, but still the argument raged because, in effect, each of the two major contenders acted as if free will could have only one meaning — his.

A simpler example of by-passing was reported by a young nurse: "I left a pan of water, soap and washcloth with a new patient, telling him it was time for a bed bath. When I returned in half an hour I found him scrubbing his bed with the cloth, but personally unwashed." While no great damage was done in either of these examples, such misunderstandings often have tragic consequences.

By-passing can come from several sources:

Multiple usage. We have an indefinitely large number of experiences and observations, but a definitely limited vocabulary. Herein lies the source of by-passing. Often the same word, in different contexts, must be used to refer to many things of the same type and to many types of things. Even the word *word*, for example, has fourteen definitions in a collegiate dictionary. *Book* can appropriately be used to refer to numerous types of printed objects, to scheduling an artist, to arranging a plane reservation, to placing a bet, to a spurious profit, to recording an arrest, or to a set of cards.

Professional training. The word *dog*, to a sawmill operator is likely to mean a clamp for holding logs in a saw carriage. To a used car salesman it may imply a beat up old car. To a layman it calls up a vague image of an animal. To a professional dog trainer it will likely mean a male of the species *canis familiaris.*

Personal experience. Everyone has a somewhat different meaning attached to a given word even when there is a clear and limited context free from the preceding problems. We know that no two people perceive quite the same object, even when stimulated by the same thing. Consider what may happen when two people look at a dog. Each sees a shaggy tan creature. One notices big teeth and barking; he feels frightened. The other notices a waving tail; he at once puts his hand down to stroke the creature's head. Each sees a different "dog," based on his past experiences. Personal experience is by far the most common source of by-passing, and the most likely to lead to trouble since it is based on affective valuation.

What can a discussant do to prevent or correct by-passing?

1. *Be person centered rather than word centered.* When you listen, look beyond the words for the speaker's meaning; when you speak, consider what the listener might mean when he uses a word you are about to use. "What would it mean if I were in his position?" "Is my interpretation of his language consistent with other things I know about him?"

2. *Question and paraphrase.* When there seems to be any possibility of by-passing, ask for clarification. Try putting what you understood into your own words, and ask if that is what the speaker meant. When you have spoken an important message, encourage paraphrasing and questioning by the listeners; sometimes you may even insist on it.

3. *Consider the context.* Note what preceded and what follows. How does your present interpretation fit with other things you have heard the person say?

Ambiguity

Ambiguity results when words are used to refer to a class of objects or to a broad category which includes several classes of objects. Semanticians talk about differing *orders of abstraction* in the use of words. For example, consider the following statements, each of which is more abstract (and ambiguous) than the one which preceded it:

a jar of "Squishy" peanut butter on a shelf at the Brown Market
"Squishy" peanut butter
spreads
food
commodities
merchandise

In the first instance, the picture in the speaker's head is likely to be very similar to the picture that results in the head of the listener. But when we talk about "spreads"" or "food" or "merchandise," we can mean many things, and the result is likely to be pictures in the heads of speaker and listener which differ significantly. Only first order, descriptive statements are free of ambiguity.

In discussions, many of the statements are necessarily highly abstract, and much misunderstanding can occur. We need to be on guard for such misunderstanding and be ready to call for less ambiguous statements if the confusion is to be cleared up. Ask for and give examples and descriptive details. For example, one discussant stated, "Lecturing is a poor method of teaching." Another responded, "Oh, no it isn't." An argument set in until a third discussant asked for some examples (lower order abstractions). The speakers were able to agree on specific cases of effective and ineffective lecturing. With the ambiguity reduced by these examples, agreement was reached on a less abstract statement which went like this: "Lecturing, if well organized, filled with concrete materials and done by a skilled speaker, can be an effective means of presenting factual information or theoretical concepts. It is usually less effective for changing attitudes or thinking skills."

Vagueness

Vagueness results either from saying too little, perhaps imprecisely, in very abstract terms or from lack of a clear picture in the mind of the speaker. What, for example, might be the meaning of a discussant who says, "Democracy and freedom are synonymous" or "Sharing in decision-making produces frustration." Quite likely he would be hard pressed to tell you. Such statements are neither true nor false — they are vague.

What can you do to reduce confusion which results from vagueness? Ask the speaker to describe what he is talking about. Perhaps some synonyms will help reduce the area of possible meaning. Verbal definitions may help a little, but remember these are only verbal equivalents, and may be more meaningless than the originally vague term. Examples may help both speaker and listener to clarify their meanings. Finally, instead of beginning a discussion with a rather vague question, you can often prevent confusion by introducing a case description of a specific problem, including many details of what happened.

Stoppers

Certain ways of talking serve as *stoppers* to the discussion process. They tend to get emotional reactions, reducing the thinking component of discussion. Stigma words, clichés and the mood of dismissal are especially likely to stop consideration of an issue.

Stigma Words

We will consider first the word *stigma* and how discussants may react to such a word. The term is used to derogate or ridicule. Notice how it works. One discussant describes an incident, expresses his point of view or suggests a solution. Another participant says: "Why that's nothing but a _____ !" "You're proposing _____ !" "We tried that and found it to be _____!" "That's _____!" In the blanks may go any word or phrase which is used to label something strongly disliked or feared, and for which most people have a highly unpleasant connotation: *communistic, socialistic, Federal control, beatnik, childish, stupid, anti-American, radical, reactionary, ridiculous,* or any words used in derogation. The first speaker has now been identified with something ugly or fearful. He may stop cold, deny and argue or call the speaker some ugly name. The group will likely get caught up in an argument over whether or not the subject of discussion should be called by the stigma. Meanwhile, the goal of the group is forgotten; harmony is lost; feelings are hurt; members lose face. Even if the group gets reoriented, residual antagonism is likely to block cooperation: "Nobody calls me that and gets away with it!"

What can you do to prevent or alleviate stigmatizing? First, recognize that people have feelings about everything, and these feelings are not to be denied. Some labeling and stigmatizing are bound to occur when people express how they feel about things. The danger is that thinking objectively will decrease, or that speakers will become so defensive they begin to attack each other without listening to understand. By being aware of the implications and dangers of a stigma (or halo) word, a designated leader or other discussant can make a direct approach to the problem by inviting other feelings and points of view. For example, you could say: "Joe has called the Peace Corps a phony. That's one point of view. Are there any others?" "Well, Helen's feeling is that it is socialistic. Is there any other way of looking at it?" "Some of us feel it is anti-American. Perhaps others see it differently." Having obtained other points of view, one can then ask for a description of the proposal or idea and how it would work. By this means talk will be once more directed to the goals of the group and the facts of the situation.

If no one is ready or willing to express a point of view contrary to that of the stigmatizer, the designated leader can sometimes help remove the roadblock to objectivity by playing the devil's advocate. In so doing, he expresses a point of view contrary to that of the stigmatizer, indicating that it is not necessarily his own but one that ought to be considered in order to objectively consider the proposal from other points of view and on its own merits. For instance he might say something like: "Joan has called the loan fund socialistic. Let's consider another judgment which I've often heard expressed by (name and source). They say it helps students develop independence. . . ."

You might also remind the group of such examples as the following: When social security was first proposed, many people opposed it as socialistic but no one now seriously proposes abandoning it; the Federal Postal Service was likewise labeled, as were programs to aid farmers and colleges.

Clichés

Another frequent stopper is the *cliché*, or proverb. It is easy to say, "A stitch in time saves nine" or "A penny saved is a penny earned, you know." These sayings seem so obvious that no one may bother to look further at the details of a proposal clobbered by a cliché. The wheels of group thinking grind to a halt on the cliché.

How can you undo the effects of a cliché? First, keep in mind that no two situations or problems are identical. Second, be on guard for easy answers, proverbs, or clichés with their stopping effects. When you spot one, you can point it out as such and suggest an examination of the details of the new proposal, especially to discover if it is different from any other. For example, you might say, "That seems too

pat. Are there any differences between this proposal and . . .?" Sometimes you can counter a cliché with another proverb, or cliché; every
cliché seems to have an antithesis. For instance, if someone says,
"Don't put off till tomorrow," you might counter with, "True in some
cases, but also remember that 'haste makes waste.' Now why don't
we look further into this proposal?"

Dismissal

Perhaps the deadliest pitfall to group communication is the *mood
of dismissal*, or *allness*. It is the mood which seems to say, "This isn't
worth considering," "It won't work," or "My mind is made up. Don't
confuse me with the facts." Common to all forms of dismissal is the
wish — perhaps unconscious — to stop communication about an idea.
As Lee described it, this is the mood in which a man indicates "he wishes
to go no farther, to talk no more about something which is to him
impossible, unthinkable, wrong, unnecessary, or just plain out of the
question. He has spoken and there is little use in trying to make him
see otherwise."[1] He may declare, "We've done it another way and we
just aren't going to try something new and dangerous," "I refuse to
listen to such nonsense," "How naive can you be?" or "Let's not waste
time with that one."

Such comments display unmitigated arrogance on the part of the
speaker. He assumes he knows all there is to know or all that needs
to be known, forgetting that the world of reality is complex, constantly
changing and known to him only in part.

What can be done to offset the mood of dismissal? First, you might
try asking for other points of view, much as you would in responding
to a stigma. In a continuing group it would be well to tackle the
problem head-on, by discussing the attitude itself with the group. An
effective way to do this is to discuss specific cases of people acting
with a mood of dismissal.[2] Keep reminding the group that mutual
respect must be given if group cooperation is to be possible.

USING QUESTIONS TO IMPROVE COMMUNICATION

It has often been said: "To know how to ask the right questions is
more important than knowing the answers." The importance to group
discussion of asking relevant, meaningful questions has been stressed

---

[1]Lee, *op. cit.* p. 46.
[2]Such cases can be found in William Haney, *Communication: Patterns and Incidents* (Homewood, Ill.: Richard D. Irwin, Inc., 1960), and in Irving J. Lee,
Customs and Crises in Communication (New York: Harper and Brothers, 1954).

repeatedly in this book. The questions we ask and how we ask them are major determinants of how effective a discussion will be. This final section of the chapter is concerned with major types of questions and some of the effects they can have on communication during a discussion.

Questions raised during discussion can be classed into four broad types: (1) fact or observation, (2) interpretation, (3) value, (4) policy. Recognizing the differences when each is appropriate, and learning how to react to each is important to the skilled discussant. A confusion in the type of question and the appropriate type of answer has led to many breakdowns in communication. A productive discussion never gets stuck on one type of question, but moves readily from type to type. Learning discussions entail the first three types. Problem-solving discussions are intended to answer questions of policy, but the answers depend on answers to the other three types.

Questions of Fact

Questions of *fact* are those which ask for reports of observations of something that has occurred. The answers should be limited to such reports, without interpretation or inference being confused with fact. Confusion often arises when a question of fact cannot be answered by any observation or is responded to with a guess, hunch, theory or pet belief. A fact as such is not discussable; it can merely be reported and verified by further observation.

Meaningful (or answerable) questions of fact are those which indicate definite steps or operations by which observations can be made. Consider the following examples of meaningful questions of fact:

"What factors did the fire chief say contributed to the burning of the Martins' House?" (Ask someone who heard him, or go ask him.)

"How did Jack Diamond score yesterday on the Rorschach Test?"

"How did the psychiatrist interpret that test?"

"How fast did Brownie (the greyhound) run in the race yesterday as recorded by the electronic timer?"

Meaningful (operational) questions of fact are not discussable. If a statement accurately represents an observation, it should be accepted without discussion. Only the means of observation or accuracy of the report is discussable. The trouble comes when people begin to discuss questions which appear to be questions of fact, but are either vague or meaningless.

Vague questions are those which contain ambiguous or vague terms, and so can be answered in many ways. They can be made meaningful by replacing the ambiguous terms with lower order abstractions which point to specific objects or events. Consider the following examples:

> "How fast can a greyhound run?" (Depends on the greyhound, which greyhound, and under what conditions?)
>
> "Does it get very hot in Alabama?" (Where and when in Alabama? What temperature qualifies as "hot"?)

Meaningless questions are those which cannot refer to any observable thing or event. They cannot be answered by any known means, so there is nothing to be gained by discussing them. You can help a group by pointing this out, suggesting that the question be dropped as meaningless. A few examples should help to make this type of question clear to you:

> How many squiggles in a gallomp?" (Notice that the form is that of a question of fact, but the words refer to nothing that can be observed.)
>
> "Why did God punish the Martins by burning their house?" (Where do we look for God? How could we observe whether punishment was meant even if we find Him?)
>
> "Is Jack Diamond's psyche deranged?" (Just what do we study or observe? This could become a question of interpretation.)

Questions of Interpretation

Questions of interpretation are concerned with the meaning of a group of facts. For example, "Do we have a serious problem with crimes of violence in our city?" "Are we suffering from inflation?" "Have high school graduates improved in writing skills since 1960?" To answer any of these questions will take many facts, and the answer will be an interpretation of those facts.

Questions of Value

Questions of value call for assessment of merit or worth. No question of value can be answered without making a comparison. Something may be compared with a set of criteria, or a comparison may be made between two or more things or classes of things. For example: "Which is the safest of the American-manufactured automobiles?" "Is the use of phonics effective in teaching reading?" "Which political party has done the most to improve living conditions in our state?" All of these questions require comparisons. When individual and personal valuations are called for, it is important to remember there is no need for agreement. There is no reason to argue about personal taste, such as, "Do you like this poem?" or "Is pork or beef better meat?" Such questions may bring forth interesting opinions, but there is no reason to argue about them. A learning group has no need to agree on matters of value, but merely to understand the basis for differing answers to questions of value.

Questions of Policy

Questions of policy ask, "What should be done to . . .?" The key word in such a question is *should*. For example: "How many credits of science should be required for liberal arts graduates?" "What should we do to reduce littering in our town?" Obviously, an answer to such questions that will be acceptable to all members of a group can be found after answers to questions of interpretation and value have been agreed upon. When communication breaks down in a group trying to agree upon a solution, it is usually wise to raise questions of value, asking what criteria are actually being applied. It may also be necessary to collect more facts and interpret them. The patterns for problem-solving discussion all provide for discussion of fact, interpretation, value and policy in that order. But sometimes the discussion is too sketchy at some stage in the process of problem solving to provide a basis for agreement on a policy statement.

Many times discussion is disrupted by a breakdown in understanding due to assumptions about language or to how words are used. The ideal discussant can recognize and prevent breakdowns which come from by-passing, ambiguous terms and vagueness. He is on guard against the stopping effects of stigma, clichés and dismissal. He recognizes the differences between questions of fact, interpretation, value and policy, and makes appropriate responses to each type. He is especially careful to clarify vague questions and to stop consideration of meaningless questions. In these ways he contributes to communication and good human relations.

BIBLIOGRAPHY

Haney, William, *Communication: Patterns and Incidents,* Homewood, Ill.: Richard D. Irwin, Inc., 1960.

Johnson, Wendell, *People in Quandaries,* New York: Harper and Brothers, 1946.

————, *Your Most Enchanted Listener,* New York: Harper and Brothers, 1956.

Lee, Irving J., *Customs and Crises in Communication,* New York: Harper and Brothers, 1954.

————, *How to Talk with People,* New York: Harper and Brothers, 1952.

Chapter 8

OBSERVING AND EVALUATING DISCUSSIONS

As many writers have pointed out, the old motto "practice makes perfect" should be revised to read "practice makes permanent." So it is in discussion. Unless practice is constantly evaluated, it may result in bad habits. The means to learning is practice with analysis and evaluation leading to change in future discussions.

Constructive evaluation depends on observation and feedback of information about how a discussion group is doing. Through reading this book, listening to your instructor, and classroom practice you are developing a participant-observer orientation. Even while you are participating in discussion, a part of your attention is given to observing how you and your group are proceeding. One cannot both observe and participate in the same instant, so attention must be shifted rapidly from the content of the discussion to the processes of the group. As skill is developed in being a participant-observer, a discussant becomes more and more able to supply both the functional roles needed by the group and the feedback about what is going on. This feedback can be used by the group to change or correct any lack of information, attitudes, norms or procedures which keep the group from being as productive as it might be.

Skillful as one may become at maintaining a participant-observer orientation, he will sometimes become so involved in the interaction over an important issue that he will lose perspective. Then a nonparticipating observer will be helpful. Any group learning the skills and attitudes of discussion (such as in a speech class) will benefit from the feedback of a nonparticipating observer. The first part of this chapter describes the role of the observer, suggests how he can make himself most useful to a group and supplies him with some forms for guiding his observations. Some of these techniques and forms can be used even when no nonparticipating observer is present. The final part of the chapter considers feedback in interpersonal relations, a special type of evaluating developed by workers in the National Training Laboratory and in group therapy.

THE ROLE OF THE OBSERVER

Every student of discussion and group processes needs the experience of observing discussion groups at work. As students have remarked countless times, "It looks different when you are sitting outside the discussion." The observer can see clearly what he was only vaguely aware of while discussing. After observing other discussants, he may be motivated to change his own conduct as a discussant. It is therefore suggested that you observe as many discussions as possible. In the speech classroom, it is wise for you to change frequently from being a discussant in one group to being an observer of another.

Do not try to observe everything at once. Limit your focus to a few aspects of the discussion, perhaps at first to only one. Later, with experience, confidence and increased awareness of the dynamics of a group, you will be ready to observe without a definite focus. You will then be able to decide as you watch which characteristics of the group are most important to assess in detail. No observer can simultaneously chronicle the content and flow of interaction, take notice of various group and individual objectives, judge the information and logic of remarks, assess the atmosphere and note the organization of the discussion. If the observer tries to do so, the result is sure to be confusion which will reduce both his personal learning and his ability to give feedback to the group.

The nonparticipating observer can do three types of things, sometimes all during a single discussion: learn from the example of others; remind the group of techniques or principles of discussion they have overlooked; supply critical evaluations of the discussion. Responsibilities as reminder and critic to the group will be discussed in the following pages.

The Reminder-Observer

Often group members need to be reminded of what they already know. During interaction they may fail to notice what has been happening or to remember useful attitudes and techniques. To help them, a type of reminder-observer role has been developed. The reminder helps the group without offering any criticism. Many of your classroom discussions will be improved by having one member participate only as a reminder-observer. The reminder role should be changed from one discussion to another in order to give everyone a chance to remind without depriving anyone for a long time of the chance to practice discussion skills. Once you have developed skill in maintaining a participant-observer orientation, you will be able to act as a reminder to nonclassroom discussion groups in which you are a participant. If you serve as a model, gradually you will notice that all members of a continuing group begin to remind.

Before serving as a reminder, the following guidelines for reminder-observers should be studied carefully, and perhaps discussed with some fellow discussion students.

DO:

1. Stress the positive, pointing out what a group is doing well.
2. Emphasize what is most important, rather than commenting on everything you may have observed.
3. Focus on the processes of the group rather than on the content and issues per se.
4. Put most of your remarks in the form of questions, keeping in mind that all authority for change rests with the group. You have no authority except to remind, report and raise questions.
5. Remain completely neutral, out of any controversy about either content or procedure. You can do this by asking questions in a dead-pan manner, such as, "I wonder if the group realizes that we have discussed _____, _____ and _____ in the space of five minutes?" "Are we ready for the consideration of possibile solutions?" "I wonder if John and Amy understand each other's points of view?" "I wonder if we all understand the purpose of our committee?" "Is everyone getting an equal chance to participate?" Such questions remind the group of principles of good discussion without leveling specific criticisms.
6. Show trends and group characteristics rather than singling out individual discussants for comment (unless absolutely necessary).
7. Interrupt the discussion only when you believe the group is unlikely to become aware of what is troubling it. First give the group enough time to correct itself.

DON'T:

1. Play the critic-umpire, telling anyone he is wrong.
2. Argue with a member or the group. If your question is ignored, drop it.
3. Tell the group what they should do. You are not playing expert or consultant; your only job is to remind the group members of what they know but have overlooked.

When serving as reminder-observer, there are many things you might look for. The content of this book can provide you with a sort of check list for observing. Some specific things you might notice when serving as reminder are suggested by the following questions:

1. Are the group goals clear? What helped or hindered in clarifying them?
2. Are all members aware of their area of freedom?
3. Is the group gathering information to define the problem fully, or has it become solution-centered too soon?
4. Do members seem to be well prepared for discussing the topic?
5. Is information being accepted at face value or tested for dependability?
6. Has a plan for the discussion been worked out and accepted by the group?
7. Does the discussion seem to be orderly and organized?
8. Do discussants display attitudes of inquiry and objectivity toward information, issues and the subject as a whole?
9. To what degree does the group climate seem to be one of mutual respect and trust?
10. Do all members have an equal opportunity to participate?
11. Is the pattern of interaction open, or unduly restricted?
12. How sound is the reasoning being done by the group?
13. How creative is the group in finding potential solutions?
14. Is judgment deferred until all possible solutions can be listed and understood?
15. Does the group have a list of specific and useful criteria, and is it applying them to possible solutions?
16. While evaluating ideas, is the group making use of information from earlier parts of the discussion?
17. Are periodic summaries being used to help members recall and move on to new issues without redundancy?
18. Are there any hidden agendas hampering the group?
19. Are any norms or procedures hampering the group?
20. Are there any breakdowns in communication due to poor listening, by-passing or stoppers?
21. Is the style of leadership appropriate to the group?
22. If a designated leader is present, is he encouraging the sharing of leadership by other members?
23. Is the discussion being recorded and charted accurately?
24. Is the degree of formality appropriate to the group size and task?
25. What else seems to be affecting the group's attempts to achieve a goal?

In addition to serving as reminder during the discussion, afterward a reminder-observer may be able to help the group by leading a discussion of the discussion or by making a detailed report of his observations. At this point he can take either of two approaches, depending on what the group wants from him and his degree of expertise:

1. a reporter, who describes the meeting without judgment, diagnosis or suggestions for future meetings;
2. an interpreter, who in addition to reporting also offers his explanations for the behavior of the group as seen from an impartial vantage point.

The Critic-Observer

A critic-observer may do considerable reminding, but his primary function is as a critic. Such an observer belongs only in the classroom or training group. In some cases the critic-observer is primarily an advisor, either to the group as a whole or to a designated leader. For example, your instructor may interrupt a discussion to point out what he feels is going wrong and to suggest a different technique or procedure. After you have become a proficient observer, you might take the role of critic-advisor for a small discussion group in another speech class or perhaps even for a group in your own class.

The critic-observer usually makes a more detailed report after the discussion than does the reminder-observer. In addition to describing and interpreting important aspects of the discussion, he will express his opinions about weak and strong points of it. He may compliment the group, point out where and how it got into trouble, and even place blame or take an individual member to task. This must be done cautiously and with tact. Many students hesitate to criticize the participation of others, and some balk at accepting criticism leveled at them. Discussants can be helped to give and accept criticism by reminding them of two points: (1) All criticism should be constructive, objective, sincere and designed to help. (2) All critiques should include both positive and negative comments, with the good points being presented first. The critic-observer, of course, will look for the same kinds of group behavior as will the reminder.

TOOLS FOR OBSERVING AND EVALUATING

Any group can improve its efficiency and atmosphere by taking time out for unstructured evaluation. The designated leader is in the best position to initiate such a bootstrap operation by suggesting the group take some time to study and discuss its activity. If this is not done on some periodic basis, there is danger of its being neglected. For this reason, regular times for assessment have been built into the operations of many business, government and military groups. Also, a systematic review is likely to be more objective than one which is undertaken during a crisis. However, if group evaluation is limited to regular periods following scheduled meetings, much of importance may be forgotten. Also, taking a break for an unplanned evaluation may correct a damaging attitude or procedure before a serious breakdown can occur within the group; therefore, it seems advisable for a continuing discussion group to use both routine and spontaneous discussions of discussion (unstructured evaluation sessions).

Many tools for more formal observation and evaluation of both groups and individual discussants have been developed and reported elsewhere.[1] In this book a few of the more important tools are reported, especially those likely to be helpful for a class in discussion or fundamentals of speech. Instruments for assessing a group are presented first, followed by those for evaluating individual participants and designated leaders.

Evaluating the Group

Post-Meeting Reaction Sheets

Post-Meeting Reaction Sheets, or PMR's as they are called for short, are frequently used to get objective reactions from discussants. Since PMR's are anonymous, a participant can report his evaluations without any threat to himself. A PMR may be planned by a chairman or other designated leader, by an instructor, by a group or by the organizers of a large conference. The PMR's are distributed, completed and collected immediately following the discussion.

A PMR sheet consists of a simple questionnaire designed to elicit frank comments about important aspects of the group and the discussion. Questions should be tailored to fit the purposes and needs of the person preparing the questionnaire. Sometimes the questions concern substantive items, sometimes interpersonal matters and sometimes matters of technique and procedure. Two or more types of questions may be mixed on a PMR. Two illustrative PMR sheets are shown in Figures 1 and 2 following.

---

[1]See bibliography at end of chapter.

Post-Meeting Reaction Sheet

Instructions: Check the point on each scale that best represents your honest judgment. Add any comments you wish to make which are not covered by the questionnaire. Do *not* sign your name.

1. How satisfied are you with the *results* of the discussion?

| very satisfied | moderately satisfied | very dis-satisfied |

2. How well *organized and systematic* was the discussion?

| disorderly | just right | too rigid |

3. How do you feel about the *style of leadership* supplied by the chairman?

| too autocratic | democratic | weak |

4. *Preparation for this meeting* was

| thorough | adequate | poor |

5. Did you find yourself *wanting to speak* when you didn't get a chance?

| almost never | occasionally | often |

6. How do you feel about *working again* with this same group?

| eager | I will | reluctant |

Comments:

Figure 1

Post-Meeting Reaction Sheet

1. How do you feel about today's discussion?

    excellent_____ good_____ all right_____ so-so_____ bad_____.

2. What were the strong points of the discussion?

3. What were the weaknesses?

4. What changes would you suggest for future meetings?

(you need not sign your name)

Figure 2

The results of the questionnaires should be tallied and reported back to the group as soon as possible, either in printed form or by posting on a blackboard or chart. The results then become a guide for review of past practice and for planning new practices. The questions must be designed to produce data which can readily be tabulated, summarized and reported.

Interaction Diagrams

A diagram of interaction made by an observer will reveal a lot about the relationships among members of a group. The diagram can reveal who is talking to whom, how often each member participates orally, and any dominating persons. A model interaction diagram is shown in Figure 3. Notice the data at the top of the sheet; the names of all participants are located around the circle in the same order in which they sat during the discussion. Each time a person speaks an arrow is drawn from his position toward the person to whom he addressed the remark. If he speaks to the entire group, a longer arrow points toward the center of the circle. Subsequent remarks in the same direction are indicated by short cross marks on the base of the arrow.

INTERACTION DIAGRAM

frequency and direction of
participation

Group_____

Time_____

     Begin _____

     End _____

Place_____

Observer_____

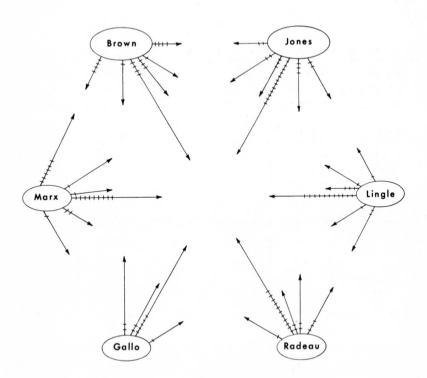

Figure 3

Rating Scales

Rating scales can be used by critic-observers to record their judgments about any aspect of the group and its discussion, including group climate, cohesiveness, efficiency, satisfaction, degree of mutual respect, organization of discussion, adequacy of information and the like. A five-point scale is adequate for most purposes. A discussion class can profitably prepare and use its own scales to evaluate a variety of group characteristics. Two or more observers working independently of each other can rate each group and then check the similarity of their ratings. Whenever ratings on the same scale are more than one point apart, the observers can learn by discussing the reasons for their different ratings. Sample scales are shown in Figure 4, illustrating how you can construct your own.

DISCUSSION EVALUATION

Date_____   Group_____

Time_____   Observer_____

Group Characteristic	5 excellent	4 good	3 average	2 fair	1 poor
Organization of discussion					
Equality of opportunity to speak					
Group orientation, mutual respect					
Listening to understand					
Evaluation of ideas					

Comments:

Figure 4

Evaluating Individual Participants

Almost any aspect of individual participation can be evaluated by preparing appropriate forms. An analysis of roles of members can be made by listing the names of all members in separate columns on a sheet on which the various roles described in Chapter 2 are listed in a vertical column at the left side of the sheet (Figure 5). Each time a

DISCUSSION ROLES

Date_____   Group_____

Time_____   Observer_____

	Roles	Participants				
Group Task	1. Initiator					
	2. Information seeker					
	3. Information Giver					
	4. Opinion Seeker					
	5. Opinion Giver					
	6. Coordinator					
	7. Orienter					
	8. Energizer					
	9. Procedural Developer					
	10. Recorder					
Group Maintenance	11. Supporter					
	12. Harmonizer					
	13. Tension Reliever					
	14. Gatekeeper					
	15. Blocker					
Self-Centered	16. Aggressor					
	17. Recognition Seeker					
	18. Confessor					
	19. Playboy					
	20. Dominator					
	21. Special Interest Pleader					

Figure 5

participant speaks, a tally is made in his column after the role function he has performed. If he performs more than one function in a single speech, two or more tallies are made. The completed observation form will indicate what functions were supplied adequately, who took harmful roles, what was the degree of role flexibility of each participant in the discussion and so forth.

Figure 6 shows a simple rating form which can be completed by a critic-observer for each participant. The forms can be filled in near the end of the discussion and then handed to the participants. This form was prepared by a group of students and has been used extensively to rate students engaged in practice discussions. Although only illustrative of many types of scales and forms which could be used, it has the virtue of being simple and brief, yet focuses on some of the most important aspects of participation.

All of the previously described observation forms and rating scales can be used to analyze and appraise functional leadership. However, because most discussion groups have a designated leader and because his participation is so vital to the group, many special forms have been developed for recording and evaluating the behaviors of designated leaders. The form shown in Figure 7 is one of the most comprehensive for evaluating designated leaders. The author adapted it from a form originally prepared for rating conference leaders in the Air Force.[2]

---

[2]Department of the Air Force, *Conference Leadership*, Air Force Manual No. 50-08 (Washington: Department of the Air Force, 1953), pp. 5-6.

PARTICIPANT RATING SCALE

for _____   Date_____

_____

(name)   Observer_____

1. Did he make useful *substantive contributions to the discussion?* (well prepared, supplied information, adequate reasoning, etc.)

5	4	3	2	1
Outstanding in quality and quantity		Fair Share		Few or none

2. Did he contribute to *efficient group procedures?* (agenda planning, relevant comments, summaries, self-discipline)

5	4	3	2	1
Always relevant, aided organization		Relevant, no aid in order		Sidetracked, confused group

• 3. How constructive and cooperative was his *attitude?* (listen to understand, responsible, agreeable, group centered, open-minded)

5	4	3	2	1
Very responsible and constructive				Self-centered, stigmas

4. Did he *speak* well? (clear, to group, one point at a time, concise)

5	4	3	2	1
Brief, clear, to group				Vague, indirect, wordy

5. How *valuable* was he to the group? (overall rating)

5	4	3	2	1
Most valuable				Least Valuable

Suggestions:

Figure 6

Date_____   Leader_____

Time_____   Observer_____

Instructions: Rate the leader on all items which are applicable; draw a line through all items which do not apply. Use the following scale to indicate how well you evaluate his performance:

> 5 — superior
> 4 — above average
> 3 — average
> 2 — below average
> 1 — poor

Leadership Style and Personal Characteristics

_____Was the leader poised, calm and self-controlled?
_____Could he be heard and understood easily?
_____Did he show enthusiasm and interest in the group and problem?
_____Did he listen well to other participants?
_____Did he show personal warmth and a sense of humor?
_____Was he objective and open-minded to all ideas?
_____Was he resourceful and flexible in handling suggestions from members?
_____Did he create a permissive atmosphere?
_____Did he make it easy for all members to share in functional leadership?
_____To what degree was he democratic and group oriented?

Preparation

_____Were all physical arrangements cared for?
_____Was his preparation and grasp of the problem thorough?
_____Did he have questions prepared to guide the discussion?
_____Were members notified and given adequate guidance for preparing?

Procedural and Interpersonal Leadership Techniques

_____Were members introduced and put at ease?
_____How well did he introduce the problem and supply necessary background?

Figure 7

_____Did he guide the group to a thorough investigation and under-
standing of the problem?

_____Did he suggest a suitable organization or pattern for group think-
ing?

_____Were members encouraged to modify his plan or agenda?

_____Did he state questions clearly?

_____Did he rebound questions to the group (especially requests for his
opinion)?

_____Did he make appropriate attempts to clarify communication?

_____Did he keep the discussion on one point at a time, encouraging the
group to complete an issue before going to another?

_____Did he provide summaries needed to remind, clarify and move the
group forward?

_____Were reticent members encouraged to speak without being co-
erced to do so?

_____Did he stimulate imagination and creative thinking?

_____Were aggressive members controlled with skill and tact?

_____Were misunderstandings, conflicts and arguments handled prompt-
ly and effectively?

_____Did he determine group consensus before moving to each new
phase of the discussion?

_____Were important information, ideas and agreements recorded ac-
curately?

_____Were plans made for follow-up and future meetings?

Figure 7 (Continued)

Observer-evaluators are not often available outside of the classroom.
Designated discussion leaders, if they are to become more proficient,
should evaluate their own participation as a means to improvement.
The questionnaire in Figure 8 may be used to evaluate one's own leadership. Many students of discussion and conference leadership have
found it helpful to complete this form after practice discussions.

FEEDBACK IN INTERPERSONAL RELATIONS

A special type of feedback and personal evaluation for group members has been developed, primarily by workers in the National Training
Laboratories of Bethel, Maine.

In this connection, *feedback* is defined as information given to a
person by another (or others) about how the other has perceived him

Self-Rating Scale for Discussion Leaders

Rate yourself on each item by putting a check mark in the "Yes" or "No" column. Score: five times the number of items marked "Yes"; 95, excellent; 85, good; 75, fair; below 75, poor.

	YES	NO
1. I prepared all needed facilities.	___	___
2. The meeting was started promptly and ended on time.	___	___
3. I did all I could to establish an informal, permissive atmosphere.	___	___
4. I had a plan for leading the group in an organized discussion of all major issues or phases of the problem.	___	___
5. Everyone had equal opportunity to speak, and participation was widespread.	___	___
6. I clearly oriented the group to its purpose and area of freedom.	___	___
7. Discussants listened well to understand all points of view.	___	___
8. The discussion was focused on the problem before solutions were considered.	___	___
9. All questions of judgment were rebounded to the group.	___	___
10. My questions were clear and brief.	___	___
11. Order and control were maintained throughout.	___	___
12. All tangents were detected promptly and pointed out.	___	___
13. Time was well distributed among all phases of the discussion.	___	___
14. All important information, ideas and decisions were promptly and accurately recorded.	___	___
15. Summaries were used to clarify, test for agreement and make transitions.	___	___
16. Unclear statements were promptly clarified.	___	___
17. I remained neutral during all constructive arguments.	___	___
18. I did everything possible to stimulate creative thinking.	___	___
19. Members were encouraged to evaluate evidence and ideas.	___	___
20. The discussion was concluded well, with appropriate planning for action or subsequent meetings.	___	___

Figure 8

and been affected by him. This permits the recipient of feedback to compare the responses of others with the responses he intended to get. He can also compare his self-image with the image others hold of him. The recipient often finds that others see him very differently from how he sees himself. Like a mirror, the feedback shows him how he is perceived along such dimensions as active - passive, agreeable - disagreeable, dependent - independent, warm - cold, cooperative - antagonistic or helpful - harmful. He may think of himself as warm and friendly, while other group members see him as aloof and cold, or everyone may perceive him differently. Since self-images are built upon what we think others think of us, such feedback can modify a participant's image and feelings about himself, thus increasing confidence, decreasing dogmatism and so forth.

Under such headings as T-group method, sensitivity training, or group laboratory in human relations a collection of individuals are put together for a period of time (from a long weekend to as long as three weeks). Sometimes members of the same company will meet for two- or three-hour sessions over a period of several weeks. Gradually the collection develops into a group, complete with a structure of roles, norms, history, culture and the like. The trainer usually limits talk to the "here and now," excluding any extensive discussion about incidents which occurred outside the training group. The emphasis is on what happens during the development of the group and interpersonal relations among the members. This focus produces a great amount of feedback among the participants. A climate of trust and frankness develops, making it relatively easy for participants to take on new roles and try out new ways of acting in a group setting. Extensive changes in attitudes toward self and others frequently occur. Individuals come to see more clearly how they are perceived by others and to be much more sensitive to the needs, feelings and techniques of other participants. Although a class in discussion or fundamentals of speech cannot act as a full-scale T-group, it can engage in similar interpersonal feedback of the sort which characterizes a T-group.

Any extensive period of feedback in interpersonal relations should be conducted in the presence of your speech instructor or some experienced group trainer. If no experienced trainer is available, you can still benefit from limited interpersonal feedback. Many variations are possible. The important thing is for each member of the group to be free to invite or not to invite the reactions of others. What he should receive are descriptions, not of himself, but of others' perceptions of and feelings toward him. Comments should be limited almost entirely to what has happened in the class.

It is possible to set up a few general categories to guide the evaluation of each other in a feedback discussion. These criteria should not be applied ritualistically to everyone, nor should comments be limited to them. For example, on the chalkboard might be written *leadership, attitudes, preparation, speaking, acceptance of others* and *warmth*.

The following guidelines should make a feedback discussion more helpful to the discussants:

1. *Describe* rather than pass judgment. No one should feel condemned as a person. A description of one's own reactions and feelings leaves the receiver of feedback free to react as he sees fit. Avoiding the use of evaluative, emotive or stigma terms reduces the need for the recipient to react defensively. For example, rather than saying, "You were really nasty," one might say, "I felt myself growing very angry when you . . . ." And don't forget to give compliments which are sincere.

2. *Be as specific as possible.* To be told he is dominating may do a discussant more harm than good. Rather, the recipient should be told what he did that was perceived as an attempt to dominate. Give details, describing what was done and your reactions to it. For example, "When we were talking about how to proceed, I thought you refused to consider anyone else's ideas, so I felt forced to accept your suggestions, face an attack from you or leave the group."

3. *Consider the needs of the receiver.* What can the receiver hear, accept and handle at this time? A lambasting to relieve your own tension may do much harm if the needs of the receiver are not sensed and responded to. Usually you should balance negative reactions with any favorable ones you may have.

4. *Deal only with behavior the receiver can change.* For example, you would not tell a stutterer that his hesitations annoy you, or a person with a tic in his cheek that it drove you nuts! However, you might let him know that you feel he has been sulking and you don't like it when he withdraws after his suggestion has been turned down.

5. *Feedback is solicited, not imposed.* Let the recipient invite comments (unless you respond immediately after he has said or done something). If he indicates he wants to hear no more, stop. He is not likely to accept what you say anyway.

6. *Check to see if your feedback is understood.* Did the receiver understand what you meant? Watch for his reactions, perhaps asking him to restate your point.

7. *See if the others agree with you.* You may find that other participants do not respond as you did to a particular participant. Questions like,

"How do the rest of you feel about that?" should be asked often.
When no one else agrees, try to find why!

8. *Expect slow moments.* At times there will be a lot of hesitation and
   fumbling. A group may be very hesitant to express its feelings
   openly. It may take a long time for frank feedback to develop.

Feedback can be especially useful after discussion of a problem
directly involving the group, such as, "What should be the date and
type of our final exam?" or "By what policy should this class be graded?"
Feedback can be especially helpful between friends and within families, sometimes under the heading of a gripe session. Indeed, no close
interpersonal relationship can develop without interchange of this sort.

No matter how it is done, it is essential that as a student of discussion you have opportunities to observe and evaluate group discussions. The less your experience and skill, the more help you will
get from observation guides and forms such as are presented in this
chapter. Planning forms for your own purposes can be almost as educational as the observing itself. Interpersonal feedback can be used as
a means of giving and getting observations. The end result of all these
techniques for observing and evaluating should be greatly heightened
awareness of what is happening in any group and greater sensitivity to
the actions and reactions of yourself and others. In short, you will have
become a participant-observer.

BIBLIOGRAPHY

Barnlund, Dean C., and Haiman, Franklyn S., *The Dynamics of Discussion,*
    Boston: Houghton Mifflin Company, 1960.
Beal, George M., Bohlen, Joe M., and Raudabaugh, J. Neil, *Leadership and
    Dynamic Group Action,* Ames, Iowa: The Iowa State University Press,
    1962.
Cortright, Rupert L., and Hinds, George L., *Creative Discussion,* New York:
    The Macmillan Company, 1959.
Smith, William S., *Group Problem-Solving through Discussion* (rev. ed.),
    Indianapolis: The Bobbs-Merril Company, Inc., 1965.

INDEX

DATE DUE

7.24 '80	
7.26.84	
2. 5.'86	
2.26 '86	
5.13.'87	
FEB 14 '90	
Ref 2/24/90	